'There are the books that touch you. Then there are the books that open out their arms and straight out hug you – *How We Met* is this second kind of book. Honest, joyful, at times heart-breaking, at times laugh-out-loud funny, but always generous in its telling . . . this is Huma Qureshi, heart and soul.'

Ami Rao, author of *David and Ameena*

'A fearlessly honest memoir of courage, love and loss, and trying to find your place in the world. Quietly heart-breaking but life-affirming too.'

Kia Abdullah, author of *Take It Back*

'*How We Met* is a wonderful read . . . a memoir of grief, becoming and true love. Huma Qureshi is a writer with a sharp eye and a romantic heart.'

Katherine May, author of *Wintering*

'*How We Met* is the book I, and countless women of simi-lar heritage, have been waiting our whole lives for. I cried, and laughed out loud as I recognised myself in so much of Huma Qureshi's story . . . It's about being the child of immigrants, it's about dreams, about motherhood, and it is about familial love, in its many forms. It's such a beau-tiful book of quiet confidence, and deserves to be read widely. Huma is a huge talent, and a skilful storyteller with an eye for an exquisite turn of phrase.'

Saima Mir, author of *The Khan*

HOW WE MET

A MEMOIR OF LOVE AND OTHER MISADVENTURES

HUMA QURESHI

Elliott&Thompson

First published 2021 by
Elliott and Thompson Limited
2 John Street
London WC1N 2ES
www.eandtbooks.com

ISBN: 978-1-78396-541-0

9 8 7 6 5 4 3 2 1

A catalogue record for this book is available from the British Library.

Typesetting by Marie Doherty
Printed by CPI Group (UK) Ltd, Croydon, CR0 4YY

Take down the love letters from the bookshelf,
the photographs, the desperate notes,
peel your own image from the mirror.

DEREK WALCOTT
'Love After Love'

For Suffian, Sina and Jude

A NOTE FROM THE AUTHOR

The past is always remembered differently,
depending on who is remembering; this is my version.

THESE DAYS

M y six-year-old son Suffian has a friend at school whose parents apparently met on the Piccadilly line on the way to work. Suffian announces this while eating his dinner in the out-of-context way six-year-olds and their ilk are prone to do. 'Charlie's parents met on the Piccadilly line and then they got married,' he says, with knowing authority.

I am sceptical. Things like this don't actually happen in real life, I tell him.

'Are you sure?' I ask.

'Yes. They met on the Piccadilly line and then they got married. They are the Piccadilly People. Charlie told me,' he says triumphantly.

The detail, for a six-year-old, is specific (it was definitely the purple line, of that he is certain) so I suppose it might be true. Perhaps Charlie's parents really do call themselves the Piccadilly People, perhaps they really did meet across a crowded Tube carriage many years ago.

'That's nice,' I say, because it *is* nice when two people come together in the universe, even if it is in a crowded Tube carriage.

'What line did you and Dada meet on?' Suffian asks expectantly. I understand from his hopeful expression that he now believes that everybody's parents must have met on the Tube. 'Was it the Northern line?' he asks, because we live off the Northern line and it is by default his favourite.

'Ah, so we didn't meet on the Tube,' I say, shaking my head.

'You didn't?'

'No. Most people don't marry people they meet on the Tube. Most people don't talk on the Tube. Most people don't even make eye contact on the Tube.'

'So where did you meet?' he says.

We've never had this sort of conversation before. His curiosity suggests that perhaps he has some sort of understanding that we were people before he and his two younger brothers came along; this feels like a turning point. But right now I don't know how to answer his simple question because there's the story of how we met and then there's my mother's version of how we met and then there's everything that happened before and also in between. I don't know where to begin.

'Well,' I say, 'technically, we met in a coffee shop.'

'And then you got married?'

'Not straight away.'

'After coffee?'

'No.'

'But you don't like coffee.'

'No.'

'Then when?'

'Later. It was . . . complicated.'

'What does that mean?'

I tell him to finish his dinner.

I text Charlie's mum. She has no idea what Charlie's talking about. They met at work.

~

Sometimes when I'm upset, when things don't work out the way I had hoped they would, I find myself wanting to gather my children in my arms and hold them close. I tell them that I love them, that I want them to know that they can be whoever they want to be, love whoever they want to love, do whatever they want to do.

My children are still very young and so they aren't yet embarrassed by such affection, often seeking it out and instigating it themselves. They respond to my fervour with their arms flung tightly and hotly around my neck and I breathe them in the way you do when you don't want to let someone you love go.

My declarations are randomly announced and often out of context. But somehow it feels urgent for them to know how far my love stretches, no matter how mundane the moment or what we might be doing at the time. It feels urgent for me to say these things, again and again, so that they will always know.

'You are my sun, you are my moon, you are my earth,' I say over dinner, pointing to each of their three faces in turn.

'WE ARE YOUR UNIVERSE!' four-year old Sina, the middle one, clamours back, punching the air like the superhero he is.

'I love you to infinity,' I say at bedtime.

'INFINITY NEVER ENDS!' Suffian shrieks. 'INFINITY GOES ON AND ON AND ON!' He jumps on the bed.

And so it goes, on and on and on.

~

Suffian still wants to know how we, his parents, met and now Sina does too. I deflect their questions and ask them instead what they think marriage means. Sina doesn't know but says he will marry me anyway. Suffian says: 'It means that you love someone and that when you love someone, it means you're going to live with them forever.' He asks me if he's right; I tell him he is. He tells me he wants to live with me forever. I tell him I'd love that but that I also completely understand if he ever changes his mind.

~

My friend Saima says: 'You should write about how you two met. You should write about how it happened.' I laugh and tell her it's really not that interesting. Besides, as parents of three small boys all we do is watch Netflix and eat dinner on the sofa once the kids are in bed. 'But people need to hear that you can break the rules and live happily ever after,' she says, in earnest. 'Women, girls like your younger self, they need to know it's not impossible.'

I laugh it off again. I don't think of myself as particularly rule-breaking. All I did was fall in love unexpectedly. See – I married Richard, someone I wasn't technically supposed to because he wasn't from my background and didn't share my cultural or religious heritage. After so many years it is easy for me to belittle this now, forget what it felt like at the time. It is easy to think of it as not even that big a deal anyway, as though telling my family about him wasn't the most difficult thing I'd ever done. Lots of people have done what I did; I was certainly not the first. I tell myself that how I met Richard is unextraordinary and normal and therefore an unimportant story to tell. But later, I catch myself thinking of us and of our marriage and our children and of the life we are making together. I look around me and I allow myself to think of what it took to reach this moment and that's when I realise:

it does matter. I ask myself: what if my story, our story, might count? What if it might mean something?

Though there is plenty of the everyday in our story, because we are ordinary and watch Netflix and eat dinner on the sofa, it does not make it any less of a great love. Though the way in which we met was normal for the time, it doesn't mean the stakes didn't feel impossible or too high to scale when we were in the midst of trying to figure out what it all meant. It doesn't mean it didn't feel extraordinary, because it did. Perhaps no one would know to look at us what it took for us to be together. Perhaps parenting has left us too tired for it to show. We have been married for nearly ten years now. I notice the soft crinkles around his blue-grey eyes, count the silver strands that appear as if by magic in my dark hair, and it strikes me that we are growing older together. This astonishes me. I realise how in the ordinariness of the everyday the steadfastness of love is revealed.

I think about what Saima says. I remember how, when I didn't know what to say to my family, I looked everywhere for a version of my story, something that might have helped me find the words I needed. I think of all the little questions my children have, and all the bigger questions that are yet to come. I wonder if they will understand that the story of how their father and I met is not so much about the specifics of when and where as it is about me, learning how to find the words I needed, figuring out what I felt, saying what I had to say even when I felt my voice falter.

~

For the longest time, our story has gone like this: we met in Tinderbox, a high-street coffee shop in Angel, long since closed, I believe. The story goes that he was stood in front of me in the line and I took his green tea by accident. He asked for it back and I said something like 'Oh god, I'm sorry, that's embarrassing', and he said, 'Not at all', and that's how we started talking. The rest, we say, is history.

Except it's not. That's not really how we met at all. I mean, it happened, we did go to Tinderbox and I did accidentally take his green tea instead of my breakfast one, and that really is what we said to each other, but it's not quite the meet-cute it has been made out to be. It's easy to get carried away, to start believing that we met by chance as if somehow that makes it more romantic. When friends, people our own age, ask us how we met (and it is surprising how many couples ask this of each other), they say things like how lovely it is, how rare for something like that to happen in such a vast place as London, like the Piccadilly People I guess.

I like this version of our story even though it is not strictly true. I like it because it implies a twist of fate. I like it because telling our story in this way also makes it less my fault. It means meeting Richard happened to me by accident, not that I made it happen by choice.

~

When our engagement was announced, my mother told some of our family and family friends that I met Richard in Regent's Park mosque as if we both just happened to spend all our free time there. She said this, I think, in order to stress that his conversion to Islam was authentic and, perhaps more importantly, to stress that my behaviour was beyond reproach, to dampen gossip in the fairly conservative, relatively strict social circle that raised me and to put a stop to the question of what other people might think and say. If I met my husband-to-be in the mosque, it meant that I was a good sort of Muslim woman, and therefore my character came out of all of this intact.

Honestly though? The truth, the very unspectacular truth, is we met online. Of course we did. How else?

EARLY MARCH, 2011

I meet Richard for the first time on a Tuesday after work. It's the beginning of spring in London. A cold chill runs through the sky, still bright and blue in the unwind of an early evening. We agree to meet outside Angel Tube station. I arrive early because I'm nervous.

I keep checking the time. Before leaving my flat, I consider what I might wear a thousand times. I'm more nervous about meeting Richard than I have been about meeting any of the strangers I've been set up with in the past through my mother, the Muslim internet, a South Asian matrimonial agency once featured in Metro, and the women I call aunties even though they are not related to me. One of these aunties sends me a sheaf of printouts of Arabic prayers in the post with a note that says if I read them seven times a day for three months, I will be bound to find someone. I wonder why she took the trouble to post the printouts to me instead of just emailing them.

Some of these aunties haven't even met me, yet they have such faith in their powers of matchmaking that they reassure my mother that they can find someone, anyone, suitable even for a girl like me. I am almost thirty, only five foot two inches tall, I'm not a doctor and I can't speak Urdu, at least not very well. My pickings are slim. I am not in high demand.

Most of the boys I am set up with are always in such a rush, always planning their next move. They send texts full of complicated abbreviations on the go and then want to meet the next day, no time to talk on the phone let alone send an email, their eyes darting fast and sharp around whichever restaurant or cafe we happen to be in, telling me before I've finished my tea that I'm not a long-term prospect, then moving on to the next girl.

But Richard and I have been writing to each other every single day for almost a month now, though we have not yet spoken on the phone. We write long, detailed emails with no emojis or abbreviations, emails which he composes perfectly, with paragraph breaks and an excellent command of grammar. I come to think of these emails as letters. As a writer, I appreciate the time and effort he makes to sit down and write, share the details of his day with me. There is something lovely about this. I find myself refreshing my inbox, waiting for his next email. We only swap phone numbers the day before we are due to meet. But I already feel as though I know him. I like everything about him. When I write to him, I feel as though I can tell him anything about myself. I also know that this sounds weird. It is 2011 and though internet dating is not unusual and there are already eHarmony adverts on TV, it is still something that people don't like to admit to for fear of looking desperate. There is still the perception that internet dating is risky because you might end up with a psycho or someone a lot shorter than their profile states.

Most of all, I am nervous because even though I have been set up more times than I'd care to remember in the last five to seven years, I've never met someone who isn't Asian. Someone who doesn't share my family heritage, my skin colour, my cultural background or my faith. All of those so-called dates were legitimate because they were halal; I was only meeting boys who understood that these meetings were fast-track interviews to marriage and that there'd be no messing around. I am nervous because I know I can't let myself like Richard. Richard is definitely not what my mother would consider a suitable boy. Technically I shouldn't be meeting up with him at all. I remind myself that he started it. It is not as though I deliberately went out of my way to find someone who wasn't from my background. I had tried the Muslim-specific matrimonial and 'halal dating' websites but let's just say I didn't have much luck. Any luck, in fact. So I thought I might have a better chance of finding someone who was still Muslim but also just a little bit more like me on a more regular sort of website. Or, as my brother's friend Mo once said, a 'middle of the road' sort of Muslim. I tell myself the onus is on him. He was the one who messaged me, and my profile clearly said I'm Muslim. Surely he must know what he's letting himself in for.

My best friend KK texts me. KK and I met at university. She went to convent school and her Nigerian parents are as strict as my Pakistani ones, which means her experience of the opposite sex is as limited as mine.

KK: *Good luck!!!*

Me: (something along the lines of) *Don't need it. This won't be going anywhere!*

Me: *I mean, his name is RICHARD. What the hell am I doing with someone named RICHARD?*

Me: *WHAT WILL MY MOTHER THINK?*

KK: *Nothing. You haven't even met him yet.*

Me: *WHAT AM I DOING?*

KK: *Just enjoy it! Go! Go!*

The name Richard is a normal, perfectly nice English name but it is the very normality, the very Englishness, of it that bothers me. What's in a name?

Everything, I tell myself. Though I hang on to every email, each time I see his name in my inbox a tiny alarm sounds in my head, faintly but loud enough for me to hear, for it is in his name that all the small differences between us lie. I should be meeting someone called Rehan or Rahim or Raiyan, not Richard.

As it happens, my name is causing *him* some concern. Earlier that afternoon, he texts me.

Richard: *I'm so sorry, and I know this sounds really stupid, but I realise I don't know how to say your name.*
Me: *Oh! Yeah, I get that a lot. Don't worry about it.*
Richard: *I don't want to say your name wrong though.*
Me: *I do hate it when people get my name wrong.*
Richard: *Exactly why I don't want to get it wrong.*

I arrive early so that I might catch a glimpse of him before he sees me. I decide that I'll see him first, and then if I really can't go through with it, I'll slip back into the station, text him that I can't make it and go home again. I tell KK of my plan.

KK: *You can't do that.*

Me: *Why? He'll never know!*

I stand to the side and watch people pour out of the station in clusters. And then, there he is. I recognise him from his profile picture, which I may have looked at a number of times. I feel a little dizzy all of a sudden. He looks around for me and there is a frown on his face, a concern that perhaps he can't find me. He reaches in his pocket for his phone. My phone pings.

Richard: *I'm here! I'll wait for you.*

And he did.

THOSE DAYS

The idea that I would be married someday was something I understood and assumed ever since I was a girl. I had been to enough Pakistani and Indian weddings all over England and beyond to know that someday I too would be a bride, perched upon a stage with a face full of make-up in a tremendous sparkling outfit as heavy as a house, poised under bright lights, a camera zooming in on me. I don't remember it ever being explained as such but I knew the system implicitly; I just did, in the same way I understood the rules about not talking to boys or dressing in a certain way. That one day a family might come to visit and then ask my parents for my hand in marriage for their son over cups of tea and a tray of samosas was as much a fact of my life as eating breakfast, reading books, watching *Neighbours* after school.

The summer my parents first spoke to me seriously about marriage was the summer between my penultimate and final years at Warwick university. We were on holiday in Italy and had caught the train from Venice to stay in Florence for a few days. When we arrived, we stopped at a large, busy gelateria full of ornate mirrors and hundreds of flavours where the servers happened to all be young and handsome, eighteen or nineteen years old, working summer jobs. Out of the blue, my mother exclaimed in Urdu how cute the blond boy serving us was and asked if I agreed. I almost spat my gelato out in shock. We never, ever talked about things like this, which is to say we never,

17

ever talked about boys. I don't know why I remember this detail, only that it seemed significant and odd given that the next time we sat down in another cafe, just a few hours later, my parents wanted to talk to me quite seriously about getting married.

I think the conversation began with me mentioning that I was interested in studying more after my degree. I had already spent a year abroad in Bordeaux in my third year and I was tempted by the idea of returning to France for a master's after my fourth year, this time swept up by the romance of living in Paris. But then my parents interrupted and pointed out that since I was going to be graduating in the next year, perhaps it was time to start thinking about meeting some suitable boys instead of planning to go away again. There had been some interest, they said.

'But I don't want that. I don't want to be looked at like that,' I said. I felt my cheeks burn. I was annoyed and I wasn't afraid to show it; my mood darkened and I pushed away my plate stubbornly like a child.

'But this is how it is, in our culture,' they said, before insisting that they were only asking me to think about it, nothing more just yet. To be fair, they really were only asking me to think about it, but at that moment I felt cornered. I was trying to tell them about my ideas and my plans for what I might do next, but they weren't listening. As a teenager, I bristled whenever my parents reminded me of 'our culture', or told me that I couldn't do something because it wasn't 'in our culture', because it mostly felt like what they really meant was whatever it was we were talking about wasn't up for negotiation. 'Our culture' was parental shorthand for 'Don't even think about it' or 'We're not like other people.' I had early-twenty-something dreams of living abroad, of maybe even becoming a journalist one day, of writing for a living, though I had no blueprint for any of this. And though marriage wasn't part of my immediate plans, that is not to say I didn't have hopes of one day falling in love, no matter how impossible the notion seemed. I didn't know practically how this would ever happen, but that wasn't the point. The point was I had dreams, no matter how clichéd they seemed. But 'our culture' brought me back down to earth.

It felt to me, in that moment, that what my parents were asking of me was stripped of any sort of romance – and I longed for romance. It is no exaggeration to say that I spent most of my teenage life reading nineteenth-century romance novels and they'd filled my head with all sorts of notions: meaningful glances, windswept proposals. In my barely turned twenties, when all summer long KK and I emailed each other about crushes and cute boys we had noticed on the bus or on the street (the extent of our experience) who may or may not have looked like Pacey Witter from *Dawson's Creek* or Seth from *The OC*, I felt that even thinking about being introduced to someone in my parents' front room was akin to being asked to give up on the smallest of possibilities. I had absolutely no interest in marrying someone who proposed via his parents in my parents' front room.

'Are you serious? Because I'm really not ready for any of this,' I said. All my life, I understood I was to stay away from boys and not to talk to them but now it seemed I was being asked to sort of do the opposite.

'You're not a little girl any more,' they said, not unkindly. 'At some point you will have to settle down.'

I spent the rest of that day following my parents sullenly around the Uffizi, dragging my heels, wishing I was anywhere else but there with them. I was reminded about something I had read in *The Portrait of a Lady*, when Isabel found herself stuck with Ralph, having to defend her reasons for daring to turn down Lord Warburton's proposal of marriage. I looked the parts up as soon as I got home and underlined them furiously: 'I don't see what harm there is in my wishing not to tie myself. I don't want to begin life by marrying. There are other things a woman can do.' And then also: 'The other day when I asked her if she wished to marry she said: "Not till I've seen Europe!" I too don't wish to marry till I've seen Europe.' I decided to try the same tactic.

I had this idea of Paris in my head. I'd been to Paris before and there was a part of me that was swept up in what I thought was its loveliness. In my mind, Paris played out like scenes from *Everyone Says I Love You* and *Amélie*, a midnight sky lit up by swaying, unsteady fairy lights. I had this image of myself, living high in some pretty little attic room up in the clouds. I pictured myself surrounded by books, maybe even writing one. I imagined walking along the Seine at sunset, entire weekends lost in museums, watching French films in arty cinemas, perhaps even practising my French with some dreamy boy in a bookshop. It sounds like a string of clichés now but back then, to me, Paris meant simply that the world was full of possibility that I hadn't explored yet. I wanted to reach out and hold it all in the palm of my hand. I wanted to run away, only with my parents' consent.

At university there was an unspoken rule that I was to call my parents every night and go home on alternate weekends, and though I loved my parents very much, I also wanted to know who I was, who I could be, when I was fully apart from them. 'It's not you we don't trust,' they said. 'It's other people.' I craved a certain distance but I couldn't admit to this because I knew it would hurt them. All I wanted was to know that I could be someone, an adult, no matter how unprepared or terrified I was.

Meanwhile KK and our other friends from Warwick were planning to move to London after finals, applying for law conversion degrees or graduate jobs and hurtling towards stable futures, the thought of which terrified me almost as much as the idea of getting married. Though I didn't yet fully know what I wanted, I knew it wasn't any of that. I wanted an excuse to put everything on hold. I felt an urgency to open my life like a lid, peel it back bit by bit and discover where it might take me. I wanted to be free to make mistakes of my own. I wanted very much to be a writer but I had no idea how to make a living out of that. I thought studying politics in Paris might help me find a job in journalism one day as well as proving to my parents there was a point, a real purpose, to my plan. I worried that if I stayed in England I'd accidentally slip into some conventional, uninspiring graduate scheme. I imagined my dreams of being a writer would disappear.

But more than that, ever since that conversation in Florence, I worried that the closer I came to graduation without a sensible career path plotted out, the more seriously marriage might be expected of me because

I hadn't had the foresight to study something voca-
tional and line up anything else. Girls I'd grown up
with who were not much older than me were already
being introduced to suitable boys and some of them
were getting engaged even before graduation; things
moved astonishingly fast in the world of aunties, rishtas
and arranged marriages. Some of my favourite cousins,
a year or two older than me, with whom I had spent
countless carefree childhood summers in Lahore, were
already married. I thought that if I could get myself to
Paris, it might buy me some time.

What I longed for, more than anything, was to
choose what my life would be like. Paris seemed a good
place to perhaps figure some of this out. Somewhere
in the back of my mind, I understood that my parents
were most likely looking for matches for me and that
once I was married, which felt inevitable, I'd never
have this chance again.

I had arranged to rent a back room from a wealthy
landlady whose vast apartment occupied the entire

fifth floor of a grand, elegant Hausmann building in Le Marais overlooking the Seine on Quai Henri IV. She was a petite divorcee with cropped dark elfin hair and a sharp chin. I only ever knew her as Madame. I saw her apartment once, on the day I arrived. She invited me in while she fished my keys out of a drawer. Her home was breathtaking, filled with art and glass coffee tables, cut flowers and classical music, long and elegant sofas. A twisted stone sculpture sat there in her lounge, as incidental as a television. In the distance I could see the tall traceries of the Eiffel Tower and the heft of Notre-Dame rising through her windows.

My diminutive square room was across a hallway, accessed through a back door in her kitchen. It had once long ago been a servant's room and from my thin, tall window I could see only the courtyard where the bins were stored and the streaky windows of the back stairwell of the Hausmann building next door. I was not to use the elaborate caged lift, which was saved for the wealthy people with the sweeping views, but rather the service entrance around the back and the stairs.

In one corner was a single bed; in another a countertop with a plug-in hotplate, a two-cup kettle and a miniature fridge. In the other corner there was a tiny bathroom behind the sort of lavatory door you'd find on an aeroplane, into which I side-stepped to enter, and then side-stepped once more to slip into the narrow shower. A desk slotted into a slim alcove, a few shelves above. Opposite, there was a small television on top of a dark wooden cabinet, which held a few plates, mugs and a box of tarnished, mismatched cutlery. I could pace the room in four steps. I could stand in front of the hotplate, reach out and touch my bed. For all of this, the rent was ridiculously high. But I didn't mind. I didn't even mind the five flights of narrow, steep stairs up and down because this little room was exactly what I wanted. I had at once no space yet all the space in the world. It was perfect.

THESE DAYS

think I would give anything for a room of my own like that room in Paris, those long swathes of uninterrupted time to read, to write, to be alone with my thoughts.

Only now after almost seven years of raising three small children, one after the other, do I finally have a number of set hours to myself every day, hours in which I try to write. I am strict with myself. I avoid all housework; I leave cooking dinner until later. I tell myself to use these precious hours only to write and for nothing else.

We share the domestic load. Richard is a brilliant father. He is patient and loving and he always gets up in the night before me if ever one of the boys wakes up. He gets up before me in the morning too; takes care of breakfast, the school run. But even with all of this and the best of his intentions to be here and to help out, which he does, most of the childcare has fallen to me, especially in the early years. It's only now that it's starting to even out. On bad days, this makes me angry. I had a naive idea that I could simply carry on writing when my children were babies but nobody told me how impossible that would be and it's my work, my writing, that took the hit. It's me. What startles me is that we never really had a conversation about this, until it was too late. And so here I am, six years later, only just beginning to play catch-up with my younger self, pitching articles, trying to write. Sometimes I feel like it is too late.

Every morning as soon as Richard shuts the door and drops the children off at school and nursery, I promise to make the most of my time, those magical hours, but even without household chores it is not easy: everywhere I look, there are reminders of my domesticity. A basket of laundry, a basket of toys, three small beds to be made. Elsewhere a wall of smiling photographs, row upon row of children's books, more now than books of my own. How can I ignore all this? Simply looking at them reminds me of the singular role I have, and I would be lying if I said that it never felt limiting.

Some days I feel as though I am flagging, hopelessly trying to keep up with other writers, the ones who didn't put their lives on hold. Four hours a day at the dining table while the washing machine spins is not the same as a room of your own, not the same as giving yourself over to something entirely. It is not the same as that furrowed frenzy of untimed hours lost in concentration until before you know it the day has darkened and, all of a sudden, hunger pangs take you by surprise.

In Paris, I sat tucked up in that little high room and wrote poetry for a while, none of it good, and I read as much in French as I could – Marguerite Duras and Marcel Proust and Montaigne. I remember days that seemed to last forever, getting up only to turn on a dim lamp or make hot tea. But now there is always one eye on the clock and, sooner than I'd like, those four hours have gone. Some days it feels as though my hands are empty, so little there is to show for it.

But then I'm at the school nursery gates and out comes Jude, my youngest child. His hair is as gold as summer straw, his toddler face as round as a fierce full moon. I hold him close, my cheek pressed next to his flushed one and he laughs with such irrepressible delight, such glee, that everything both softens in an instant and expands into full bleed. Suddenly, the world is brighter, the day is warmer, the sky clearer, the light more dizzying. Every day, it hits me, this swell of yearning. Soon his brothers will join him and the house will shake as they stomp their feet and it is mostly chaos and someone will almost always cry but sometimes it is surprisingly calm, a steady ship, and I feel capable. At other times I feel exasperated or spent but then a small hand will slip into mine unexpectedly or hook around my neck, pull me in close for a kiss, and I feel it again: the swell, the love.

Just yesterday, Suffian tugged at my arm with some great urgency.

'What's the matter?'

'Have to tell you something!'

'Go on, then.'

'YOU'RE THE LOVELIEST PERSON I KNOW.'

'Oh! Why?'

'Just because!' He skips away.

Richard says Sina is infatuated with me. 'I want you,' he says, climbing into my lap. He was born in June when the strawberries came out and we made up a song about it; I whisper sometimes when he is calm and sleepy and smells like clementines that he is the one who makes it feel easy. 'I want you. Only you. You, you,

you,' he says, greedily jabbing his finger at me as though I am a snack he wants to eat. I kiss his nose. I forget that hours earlier all I wanted was the peace of solitude and its ensuing productivity to roll on and on, endless like a wave. Because I also want all of this too, so much.

Sometimes when we come home, my laptop is still open, my notebooks still spread out on the dining table, the cursor blinking mid-sentence at the point at which I must have looked up and realised in a panic that I had to leave right that instant or else I'd be late to pick one or all of them up. I ignore the little ache inside that sighs for just a little bit more time. 'Write about how you met,' my notebook says. 'Write about how it happened,' my friend Saima says. 'Show us happily ever after' – and I am trying my best, but time is catching up with me and it keeps running out.

THOSE DAYS

In my parents' conservative social circle of Pakistani and Indian doctors and their families, it was largely unheard of to send a daughter abroad on her own and this was the second time I had gone. No one else I knew from this part of my life in Walsall, from all our family friends, had ever done this. My parents were rather brilliant like this.

Some of the Indian and Pakistani girls I'd grown up with, my childhood friends, told me again and again how lucky I was to have parents who let me go abroad; their parents would never let them, they complained, and I felt it, the luck. My mother was born in Uganda and had grown up there, surrounded by an Asian community she always described as relatively open-minded and well-travelled, but we knew few East African Asian families in the West Midlands. Her eldest sister, my aunt, had come to England from Uganda as a single young woman to study in the early sixties. Her mother, my grandmother, a woman I'd never known for she died when my own mother was only fifteen, had made my grandfather promise that he'd educate their daughters because her own father had refused to educate her. (After their marriage, and her father's death, my grandmother studied despite having seven children and became a primary school teacher in Kampala.) My grandfather needed no convincing – he was the chief education officer for Asian schools in Uganda and founded colleges and schools specifically for the education of girls. After his death, my mother discovered he'd paid the fees for girls whose families couldn't afford to send their daughters to school in Pakistan.

Before she met my dad, my mother won funding to study for a PhD in England but she turned it down in order to stay with her father, to whom she'd become incredibly close after her mother's death. He insisted she go but she didn't; even after I was born, both my father and my grandfather kept nudging her back towards further study at university but she said, 'I have these three little PhDs now', meaning, of course, my two brothers and me.

My father came from a more traditional family in Lahore; his only sister, the eldest sibling, was never educated formally, while he and his brothers were. I imagine all of this history must have shaped my parents' attitudes, whether deliberately or subconsciously, because it seemed they wanted to give me every academic opportunity they could, especially because I was a girl. But even with my parents' approval and open encouragement, my move to Paris still made certain tongues wag back home in Walsall.

For the longest time, my parents' social life was my social life, and Walsall was at the heart of it. Every weekend there was a party to go to at some uncle and aunty's house, and often our house too. There were always far too many people invited, cars parked up the road for miles occasionally annoying the white neighbours because of someone's Mercedes half blocking a pavement or a drive, the air thick with the smell of kebabs and biryani. When we arrived at these parties, we took our shoes off and added them to the mountain overspilling at the door and then we'd file off into individual rooms – dads in one, mums in the other, the kids upstairs. At some point, invisible lines were drawn, and the boys and the girls learned to separate. The boys went off into one bedroom to play computer games or indoor cricket, and the girls were assigned another room, sometimes with a TV to entertain us, and that . . . was about it.

At the height of my teenage years, you could barely smile at a boy across the hall without someone making a huge drama out of it, sending the aunties into a spin. On the one hand, we were all encouraged to think of each other as family, to consider the children of our parents' friends as surrogate cousins because we were so far away from our real cousins, who were all in America or India or Pakistan. On the other hand, we weren't even supposed to talk to each other for too long. One of the boys once sent one of the girls a Valentine's card and this caused no end of gossip and concern among the older generation, who thought it a sign that this generation of Western-raised children had gone too far. When it was finally my turn to go to university, I was quite glad to be away.

I'd only been in Paris for a few months when Ayisha, one of my closest childhood friends, the daughter of friends of my parents, called me. 'There's something you should know,' she said. It turned out that some of the boys we were acquainted with from our parents' social circle were spreading rumours about me and why I'd gone to France. I say boys; they were a handful of men in their mid-twenties. For some reason, they decided I must only have gone to Paris because of a boy. 'They're saying you're with someone,' she said. 'Like . . . *really* with someone.'

At first I tried to laugh it off. I'd heard similar gossip before, rumours about a girl spotted somewhere she wasn't supposed to be or being too friendly with a boy or wearing a skirt that was too short, always the girl up to no good, almost always the girl's reputation at stake. Then, when the implications of what they were saying hit me, I was furious.

I was in my early twenties, old enough for it to matter, to stick to my reputation like mud. Though I shake my head and laugh about it now, and though it may not sound like much, at the time it was deeply upsetting for my parents and for me. It felt serious, because in our world, it was. 'What do you mean they're saying I'm *really* with someone? What is that supposed to even mean?' I asked Ayisha, though we both knew what the innuendo implied.

It was ridiculous. Even if there had been a boy, there was no way I would have been brave enough to do anything. Ayisha and I used to make jokes about this all the time – that even if anyone ever did ask us out (not that this was in any way remotely likely), we'd freeze from the fear of our mothers and what the aunties might say. We joked the fear was so deeply instilled in us, it would haunt us even on our wedding nights. The truth was, we'd been raised with certain Muslim values around relationships and dating before marriage, and even though I liked to admire nice-looking boys, those values meant something to me, which was why the rumour that I was *really* with someone hurt so much.

There was a time I'd been tempted to be more than just friends with a sweet boy on campus, part of the innocent drama of our twenty-something, will-they-won't-they lives. But I knew in my head that even if I let something happen, there'd always be limits. At home, my parents were considered the cool ones because they let me go to France on my own when I was fourteen to stay with a French Pakistani family we'd befriended, or to a David Bowie concert on a school night even though I was underage. But they were surprisingly strict about other things, especially clothes and boys and mixed parties, and it was hard to predict sometimes what was permissible and what wasn't. Now and again, I'd be reminded that something was or wasn't in 'our culture', but most of the time my understanding of what was 'our culture' was assumed as a given and not always explained. Once after I came home from Bordeaux, a French friend sent me a set of photos in the post which accidentally and entirely on purpose got opened by my parents before they got to me. They were the sort of pictures that summed up one wistful summer: a group of us on a balcony in the sunshine, goofy faces, a French boy's arm flung casually around me for the half-second the camera captured us. In another photo on the same balcony, I was leaning over and my T-shirt had ridden up just a sliver, if you looked closely enough, which my parents did. The discovery of these pictures meant I sulked in silence around them and it was in these silent reproaches that I understood what my limits were. Boys were to be kept at more than arm's-length as aloof acquaintances (or later, polite colleagues to talk to briskly about work). At university and even at school I'd seen the effort that a few friends with upbringings similar to mine went to in order to cover their tracks: the rehearsed covers, the excuses, the phone calls, the number of people involved in creating one small white lie. It seemed a lot of trouble to go to just to make out.

With rumours about my life in Paris gathering like rain clouds, I realised I had to say something. My parents were due to visit me in just a few weeks, something I'd been looking forward to, and I didn't want this to overshadow their trip. So I called them up one night and told them there was something we needed to talk about before they came. I asked them to put me on speakerphone, and then I told them everything Ayisha had said. They asked if any of it was true. I promised them that this imaginary boy I was supposed to have been with didn't exist, that the whole thing was nonsense. They believed me because although they enjoyed the social world they were a part of they also knew that it was sometimes a little too small in its outlook.

I had longed to experience something that was just for me, to feel the thrill of living somewhere different, to face an opportunity that might challenge me. Perhaps those weren't convincing enough reasons for some of the people back home. To someone who hasn't grown up in a world where things like an unmarried young woman's chastity and reputation matter, where boys and girls sit segregated in separate rooms at dinner parties, where the tiniest exchange is intense and emotionally charged, where teenage girls and grown women are judged for revealing their upper arms or their ankles or their calves, this may all seem trivial, but knowing that rumours about me were going around, that I was doubted, felt unbearable. Every time I thought about it my eyes stung, as though a strange fog was rolling in. I felt guilty at the distress and the worry I'd caused for my parents. I wondered why I couldn't just stay home, or at least stay in the same country, instead of always trying to get away.

I was studying politics at Sciences Po, a prestigious institution; that a girl from a Pakistani family from Walsall should have been there at all seemed at times like a small miracle to me. I was so angry that my achievement was being undermined. After our conversation, my father called the gossipmongers up one by one and told them – quite forcefully, my mother says – that it was sad they were so threatened by a girl who was, so he said, more intelligent and independent than they were. It made me feel better to think of these boys, because they were still boys even if they were older than me, being put in their place by him but I couldn't shake the feeling that even in another country I wasn't free from the scrutiny of other people.

It was a while before I could see the funny side: that everyone back home had thought I was living some sort of glamorously illicit, immoral life smoking cigarettes and drinking wine shacked up with my hot lover in Paris, when nothing could have been further from the truth. I spent most of my time outside of university on my own. The hours on my course were long and intense and at times my head hurt from the effort of keeping up. When I wasn't studying, I did small things that pleased me. I spent a lot of time browsing in bookshops. I found a little cinema in a cobbled side street that I escaped to on Sunday afternoons. I visited the Musée d'Orsay and stood in front of Degas's painting of the Bellelli family, holding my breath, studying the severity of the family's silent, stern faces. I discovered a food market in Le Marais and the satisfaction of cooking one-pot meals on my single hotplate. I met KK on MSN Messenger for late-night chats and idly replied to Ayisha's texts, which were forever commanding me to make the most of being away from home. I read long articles about Iraq in *Le Nouvel Observateur* and looked up all the words I didn't know. I window-shopped for beautiful clothes in boutiques that took my breath away and then I saved up and bought myself a navy blue silk dress, light as a ribbon, the sort of loose, poetic dress that I'd never have worn in Warwick or Walsall but somehow suited me here.

Perhaps it sounds as if I didn't make the most of Paris. But in my mind, I did. I had only wanted something for myself. Walking home from university in the breath of the cold and the dark, crossing the Pont de l'Archevêché under the creeping shadow of Notre-Dame, I felt something close to exhilarating. There was something thrilling in being alone in these unaccountable moments. I had this feeling that there was something bigger out there. Maybe I could be somebody, on my own.

Sciences Po had a journalism school and was encouraging current postgraduates to apply. I felt the good luck of one door opening after another. The timing couldn't have been better, I thought, as I filled in my application.

⁓

My parents came to visit me in Paris. It was early May, nearly my twenty-third birthday, and the city was fragrant with flowers, impossibly pretty. It is true what they say about Paris in the springtime. I have a photograph of them from that visit, sitting together on a bench in the Luxembourg Gardens, surrounded by pink papery tulips the size of giant teacups nodding sleepily in a soft breeze. They arrived with boxes of breakfast tea, tins of biscuits, birthday presents and a pile of my favourite magazines. I was deliriously excited to have them come and see me because I missed them, I really did. I wanted to show them that I had made myself a small home in this big, dazzling city. I wanted them to be proud of me and I loved knowing that they were.

During the day while I had lectures and seminars, my parents busied themselves visiting the Louvre and the Grande Mosquée de Paris and taking a day trip to visit Monet's gardens in Giverny. Sometimes in the late afternoons, they met me at the Sciences Po gates, impressed by the photographs of important politicians hanging in the halls. Often we walked back to my little room together, weaving across the Left Bank over to the Right, so I could drop my books off before they took me out for dinner and then returned to their hotel, and it was on these walks that I noticed how my father walked more slowly than he had before, always a few feet behind my mother and me. He struggled up the five flights of stairs to my room, stopping for breath along the way. He made a joke of it, pretending to mop his brow with the hankie that was always in his pocket.

It was the loveliest of weeks, the days long and bright and blue. No one mentioned marriage or suitable boys. We didn't talk about the rumours of that mysterious French lover. No one argued over the tiniest of things, and this surprises me because nowadays my mother and I both concede that if we spend longer than three days together, either one or both of us ends up annoyed at something the other has done or not done, said or not said. But this week went swimmingly. At the time, there was talk of my eldest brother getting married and my parents were preoccupied by this. I was off the hook. One night I almost told them about my plans to apply to journalism school but at the last moment I hesitated, deciding it wasn't worth bringing up unless I got offered a place, which certainly wasn't guaranteed. When I said goodbye to them at the station and they clasped me tight, I felt a certain fullness, contentment from having curled up in their company for a while. I would miss them because I finally had the chance to.

One Sunday morning a fortnight later, the phone rang early and woke me up and though my mother spoke brightly down the line, filling the first few moments with small talk, I knew something was wrong. When your parents are like my parents, when they leave the country they call home and all the people they love to set up new lives in different, strange, neat suburbs far away, you grow up knowing that a phone call in the early hours can only mean bad news. We had had those phone calls before: the one that told my father his only sister was dead, the one when my mother cried such an odd, knotted cry at the news of her father dying that I hid behind the sofa until her cry softened into silent sobs. In my half-sleep that Sunday morning in Paris, I knew something was wrong before I picked up the phone.

My father had fallen down the night before during his evening prayers. He had suffered a stroke. At the time, I didn't know what this meant or how bad it could be. My mother tried to reassure me by holding the phone up to my father so that he could speak to me, but his voice came out sideways and sloppy. The sound of him frightened me. I asked if I should come home. My mother said no, but she really meant not yet. I packed a bag anyway just in case. Later that day, one of my brothers called.

'He's asking for you. Can you come?'

I caught the first flight back to Birmingham the next day.

It was worse than any of us had thought. My father had not just suffered one stroke but a series of them, each one wiping out a little bit more of his body and his brain like a hurricane. We were told he wouldn't survive. It was as though the ground was shaking, the clouds cracked, the sky was falling down. The world went blurry. Time lost all meaning. It passed too quickly to even take a breath and yet also somehow lasted an age.

We prepared for the worst, as much as you can prepare for being told someone you love is about to die seemingly out of the blue, which is to say we cried a lot and then we stood in uncomprehending stunned silence at his bed in pairs and forgot to eat or brush our teeth. There were tubes, everywhere. Machines, blinking in the darkness of intensive care like small red eyes. At night, I spent a lot of time sitting cross-legged on my bedroom floor surrounded by empty space or else looking out of my bedroom window bewildered at the dark sky, searching for a sign somewhere in the faint stars. I felt very small in the face of something so much bigger than me. I began to pray because I realised there was nothing else left to do. It was all we had left.

But then came a moment of limbo. Somehow, my father defied the odds and steadily, shakily, began to breathe by himself again. The damage from the stroke had been done though; he was half paralysed. Given the choice to have half of my father or none of him at all, we took that half and we tended to it, as though he were a fragile bird with a broken wing. I held out a teaspoon of melted ice cream the colour of daffodils for him so that he might sip it and swallow and when he did I cried tears of both sadness and joy. Slowly, at a painful pace, we began to find some order in the rootlessness of our new life. After long weeks, we began to kiss my father goodnight at the end of the day and return home to sleep in our own beds instead of snapped over like sticks in uncomfortable hospital chairs.

My brothers went back to work in London. Though they came back every Friday night like clockwork, a small part of me watched them leave every Sunday evening and thought: 'And what about me?' I missed my exams in Paris. I told myself it didn't matter and that I didn't care, but I also did. My tutor said they'd pass me anyway given the circumstances as long as I finished my dissertation. I realised that would have to do. My mother and I spent our days at the hospital, staying longer than visiting hours allowed because the nursing staff knew my father once as a doctor and I suppose bending the rules for us was their way of showing him, and us, kindness in the face of such cruelty. We washed him, changed his sheets and his hospital gown, rubbed the angry sores on his back with cooling cream. We did what we could, what we had to do.

Eventually, with my father stable, my mother went back to work on another ward in another wing within the same hospital, so I spent each day with him, sitting by his side. Sometimes I held his hand and talked to him as brightly as I could or we watched TV or I read aloud to him from the newspaper until he fell asleep, at which point I'd read or work on my laptop, trying my best to finish my dissertation. Sometimes it was too much and I'd run out of the overheated ward, leaving the staleness behind, head in hands, a nurse calling out behind me: 'Are you okay, love?'

～

It was about this time, when my mother had gone back to work, when it felt that perhaps the worst of the storm was staved off for now, that she raised the issue of my marriage again. She sat next to me on my bed and said she wanted to talk to me about something and I immediately felt the day fall. She spoke in a measured way as though she'd rehearsed what she'd wanted to say. She told me how, the way things were, the future looked uncertain so it was better for me to settle down now, quickly. It was time to consider my prospects more seriously. I stared at the carpet until my eyes hurt.

Apparently, there had been a number of families who had asked after me, mothers enquiring for their sons, and apparently they'd been asking all the time I'd been at university but my parents had listened to what I had said in Florence and had politely put these people on hold. But I was a year older now. And things were different. She told me the details of one rishta in particular, a doctor eight years older than me who lived in a small town off the M1 a few hours away. I had never met him, but his mother knew mine from their university days in Peshawar. I listened.

My mother was right. Though my father was relatively stable, his condition could flip like a coin. A bad night, a bad set of blood results, phlegm on his chest; it all set him back. There had been no talk of my father being discharged. Although we couldn't plan for a life with my father back home yet, we could at least plan for mine. My older siblings were settled in careers and on the property ladder; things were different for them. It was my future that seemed the most uncertain and therefore the most necessary to sort out. Besides, it was not as if I had some great career mapped out. I'd left Paris in such a rush, I didn't have any idea what I was going to do next.

I suppose my mother wanted me to think seriously about getting married because here I was at home, no longer the one that lived overseas, of age and available. The longer she left it, I suppose she must have thought, the harder it would be, because that's the way it was (still is). Perhaps in the helpless situation of my father being so ill, arranging my marriage was the one thing my mother felt she could do. I understand why – I understand what it feels like to want to hold on to some semblance of control in the midst of uncertainty, to do what you can about something when you can't do much about anything. I understand all she was trying to do was what she thought was best for me.

But it wasn't the right time. Our family life was changing and I hadn't had time to process it. A version of my father may have been alive, but I was in the middle of mourning the one I had lost. After the strokes my father was unable to speak and communicated to us through blinking his eyes. It broke my heart that he was reduced to this. I missed hearing his gruff voice, his raucous laugh, his family stories which could fill up a room. I missed the annoying but funny way he used to stand on the landing in the morning singing 'Wake Me Up Before You Go-Go' very loud to get me up for school. I missed the way he came into the kitchen from the garden after having mowed the lawn in his vest, smelling like the earth, the fresh air. Now he was someone else. My dad had put a bunch of grown-up boys in their place when they started spreading rumours about me. Who would do that the next time?

The weeks were long. I missed my brothers and KK and our small group of university friends who were all in London. Like my mother, I was scared. I was frightened my father would die but I was also frightened for myself. I was scared that I might be left behind in the small town I'd grown up in where nothing much had changed. I was scared that if I stayed, I might never leave and I felt ashamed that this worried me so much, that I wanted too much. I missed my life in Paris where it felt as though my life was just getting started; one particularly morose night, I withdrew my application for journalism school and wept for everything I had lost and was losing, still. My father, my postgraduate degree. I felt guilty for even just thinking about wanting more at a time like this, for not being dutiful enough.

So I listened to what my mother said and I stared at the carpet in my bedroom and I agreed because I felt bad and guilty and I didn't know what else to do. My mother was so tired, withdrawn and small, and she was so, so worried about my dad, about me, about everything. I wished I could do something, anything, to take even a small part of her sadness away. I told my mother that I would meet the doctor she wanted me to, and that I would marry him if she wanted me to, because it was what I thought I needed to do with only half of my father alive. It was, I thought, what my mother needed to hear. I felt the weight of something sombre inside of me and I figured that was what it must feel like when you know you must do the right thing, even if it's not what you really want to do at all.

THESE DAYS

Sometimes I look back and I try to remember what it was like before my father fell ill. Mostly I remember this feeling of vastness unfurling in front of me, a lazy stretch I might just ease into, the belief that there was plenty of time for everything.

In my last week at Warwick, when my friends and I had taken down our photographs and packed up our bedrooms into boxes and suitcases and everyone felt wistful and forlorn, someone had the idea to spend a day in Stratford-upon-Avon to chase the blues of our forthcoming farewells away. When I think of my life before my father's stroke, life before having to think about marriage, it's always this day that comes to mind. It reminds me of being impossibly young. I remember the sunlight falling through the trees as we rowed a boat clumsily down the river, girls and boys, friends, together. Arms linked, hands held. I think of the dip-dip of the oars, the clarity of laughter; I think of how easy, carefree, it was. I remember the mossy water, the bowing willows, the freshness of the air, the clatter of pebbles and skimming stones. The lightness of nobody telling me what to do, of not worrying about being spotted, of what someone else would think. I think of how young and naive I was, how happy. How grown-up I felt, but how young I was. How little I knew of loss, life, love.

I had long ago learned to keep sun-dappled photos of this day and others like it in a secret place, though it still makes me a little sad to remember that I couldn't share these moments with my parents. I grew up learning how to self-edit because it's what so many of us second-generation types had to do. It's what we all did even when there was little to hide because even the smallest of things could be misinterpreted. A boy's arm around my shoulder could cross a line, so I knew better than to explain that some of my friends at university also happened to be boys, that it was possible for us to like the same things or even different things and each other's company without it meaning I was transgressing my upbringing. I knew better than to mention that some nights after my daily phone call home, I wandered down the hall and hung out with those friends-who-happened-to-be-boys in their bedrooms and we'd listen to Cake and Silverchair and Air before I'd get bored of their dull choices and make them listen to Destiny's Child or TLC or Brandy instead and we'd eat popcorn and watch illegal downloads of *24* episodes, or talk about Sartre and Sylvia Plath and a whole load of rubbish until after midnight because that's what you do when you're studying literature and philosophy and French and the world feels so big and so clever and you're still only eighteen or nineteen; or at least that's what *we* did. I knew better than to divulge this sort of thing because I wasn't supposed to be alone with a boy at all and certainly not in his bedroom, certainly not with the door closed.

I was learning to draw my own lines of what felt permissible (being friends with boys, allowing myself to crush on the cuter ones relatively guilt-free) and what didn't (alcohol, skipping Ramadan, a boyfriend) but I knew those lines wouldn't necessarily match the ones I'd been brought up with neatly or exactly. I didn't want to disappoint my parents or hurt them, but a righteous part of me also felt their inevitable reactions wouldn't be fair because what I was doing wasn't even wrong. It was just me, trying to figure out what I wanted or who I wanted to be. It was just me, trying to grow up.

In the early 2000s, we filled the drawn-out university holidays between our ten-week terms making mixtapes and writing long, lazy letters over the course of several days. At home I learned to wake up early and try and reach the post first, to tuck away the letters from those friends-who-were-boys inside my textbooks where they'd not be seen (KK's writing was entirely illegible so I didn't mind so much if her letters got found). I remember how once in the summer holidays a bunch of us, including a couple of the boys from our halls, were meant to meet up at KK's house in London for her birthday as a surprise. We were going to ring her doorbell and wave balloons and yell 'Surprise!' and then take her out for a big birthday lunch before taking our respective trains back to our hometowns. I'd organised the timings with her mum, who was going to make sure that KK was home. One of the boys phoned me on my clunky mobile phone to double check our plans and my mum came into my room for something and overheard his voice and of course I hadn't told her that there would be boys there. So I was busted. Eventually I melted her cold shoulder, pleading that it was KK's birthday, that KK was my best friend and I had to be there, that the boy I was on the phone to was more *her* friend, not mine. In the end she conceded that it was okay for me to go but not before letting me know that she expected more from me, that letting me go didn't mean that she approved of me meeting up with boys secretly in the summer holidays or speaking to them in my bedroom on the phone. I don't know if she would have been any more approving if I'd been truthful in the first place; the boys would still have been there either way.

It may sound as though I'm complaining about the tiniest of things, remembering a handful of details by which to define an entire period of my life, bemoaning the fact that I was so boy-obsessed but wasn't allowed to bring a boy home (good lord; imagine). I don't mean to sound like that. I don't want to make out like I had this awful upbringing because I really, really didn't. What I want to say is: I had a lovely upbringing and I had loving parents. And I often made my own privileged and somewhat spoilt choices – because I had choices even when I thought I didn't. I mean, take Paris. I didn't have to fight for it. In fact, when I panicked a week before I was meant to leave and told my dad I wasn't sure if I really wanted to go any more, because

I was terrified I wouldn't be able to keep up with all the others who were bound to be cleverer than me, the ones who belonged there, he told me that was just my nerves talking, that I had to go because it was such an opportunity and besides, I had a right to be there, he said; I had earned it just as much as any of the others there. Early on, I remember calling home in a state of worry because even though Paris was Paris, it was incredibly overwhelming. Sciences Po was notoriously tough on its students and at first I felt totally out of my depth, surrounded by students who, to me, seemed overflowing with confidence and were so much more intellectual than I'd ever be. But my parents (rightly) talked me into staying, telling me that I was being too hard on myself, that I shouldn't doubt myself so much. They were right to have insisted I give it some time because pretty soon there was nowhere else I'd rather have been.

But I have always doubted myself and my parents have always pulled me through. While I was writing this book, an article I wrote for the *Guardian* got spiked and I WhatsApped my mum, down in the dumps, and she replied, 'Don't be upset, Huma. You are much stronger than these small things. Life is full of ups and downs so just take this down with a smile and think positive!' Growing up, I was unable to shake this feeling of a great lack inside me, an emptiness that told me I was not good enough, clever enough, pretty enough, popular or successful enough. It still happens these days, but I'm able to talk about it a little more, and that helps me shake it off (most of the time). But when I was younger, this feeling hit me like a bus, time after time. I don't know where it came from. Once, during my final year at Warwick, I called home in what I now realise must have been an anxiety attack. I'd been in my room revising for exams but all of a sudden it felt as though the walls were closing in and I couldn't breathe. I was convinced I was going to fail, that I was going to mess everything up. Everything felt impossible; it was too much. My parents managed to calm me down, taking it in turns to talk to me, and then they made the decision to drive over and pick me up and bring me home. They have always picked me up each time I've felt I was about to fall or fail.

As a teenage girl who hated absolutely everything about herself, I slammed doors and slouched and was prone to bouts of extreme moodiness. I was stubborn and did things without thinking and with a great deal of drama (sometimes I still do). I talked back and argued whenever they asked me to do something I didn't want to do. Or if I did do it, I made sure they knew how downright miserable I was about it, like how I sulked on the flight every time we went back to Pakistan in the summer holidays. Though I wore English clothes all the time at home, my parents were funny about me wearing them in front of my Pakistani relatives and so my mum always picked a shalwar kameez out for the flight so that I wouldn't look too Western touching down the other side. The problem was that I *hated* being seen in shalwar kameez outside the house, because all I wanted to do was fit in. I absolutely hated that I had to be the one to wear something different that *everyone* could see while my brothers still got to wear jeans; as a result I barely spoke to my parents for the duration of every eight-hour flight we took there.

Maybe this is just the stuff of being a teenager. Slamming doors, shouting back, keeping secrets, testing parents' limits, pushing their boundaries and their patience (Suffian already likes to remind me that I am 'not the boss' of him). I suppose the difference is that with me my adolescence lasted beyond my teenage years and into adulthood. Sometimes even now, when I am back in my teenage bedroom, my own small children sleeping in a row at the foot of my bed on little mattresses on the floor in front of the desk where I used to sit and do my homework and dream of bigger things, I find a sort of familiar petulance rising up inside me for no reason other than because I am back home and it feels like it's 1999 and I'm in sixth form all over again, desperately wanting to be someone else.

But I could never be someone else and I guess that was the point and my biggest problem. For a while, and perhaps unfairly, I resented my parents for that. Being a teenager is universally hard but for some of us it is arguably harder. At some point I realised that I was different from the other girls at school; that I was never going to be like the girls in *Just Seventeen* who wrote letters asking for advice on their kissing tech-nique. At that age, I didn't realise that I didn't *have* to be like that in the first place to be accepted or to be happy, anyway. At some point I understood that the way things were for my English friends, the ones who could have sleepovers and wear short skirts and shave their legs, the ones who didn't have to hide phone calls or letters or friendships with the opposite sex or ask for permission from their parents quite so much, was not the way they were ever going to be for a girl like me.

THOSE DAYS

Word of my availability spread while I waited to meet the doctor. We weren't exactly exclusive and this was the way of arranged-marriage suitors; one could in theory have several potential lines of enquiry on the go at the same time. In the evenings, after we came home from the hospital, the phone would ring, distant callers asking after my father's health but then also specifically after me. I stood on the landing, listening to snippets of conversations about my height and my degree, the measure of my worth. I tried to ignore how it made me feel to be reduced to a check-list but all I could do was shut my bedroom door a little more forcefully (wonky hinges and a thick carpet denied me the satisfaction of ever slamming it properly). Some days I was so frustrated, I wanted to scream. I took up running, just to get out of the house, to feel the wind on my face, to forget the hopelessness of my father's diagnosis and my own situation, even though the two did not compare.

In Paris, I had begun to feel as though I was on the brink of something. I couldn't explain what exactly, only that I felt I was on the way to becoming someone I liked, someone capable and quietly confident, someone I wanted to be. A room full of books, a small writer's desk; Paris had signalled to me a tiny possibility of who I could be, dangled the prospect in front of me. Back in Walsall, I felt it slip through my fingers like dust. God's will, as everyone always said.

I called KK and told her about the doctor and what was happening. Since my father had been in hospital, our conversations had been much more serious, far beyond the scope of discussing *Dawson's Creek*.

'But is this how you want it to be?' she asked me.

'I think it's just the way it's supposed to be,' I said.

~

The doctor and his family came to our house to see me on a Sunday afternoon. I baked a Victoria sponge cake. The sky was bright blue and we sat out in the garden as though everything was normal. The doctor was boyish-looking and handsome with a head full of dark, shiny hair, and this surprised me. At the time, anyone over the age of thirty seemed old to me and he was thirty-one. After they left my mother gave me a Post-it note with the doctor's phone number on it, written in his mother's hand. We were supposed to talk to each other and in this way, sooner rather than later, confirm we were happy with our match.

'Maybe it won't be so bad, doing it this way,' I said to KK. 'He's actually quite handsome.' We tried to look on the bright side.

'It's sort of like having a boyfriend. Maybe?' KK
suggested, trying to lighten the mood.

I thought about it. 'Not quite, I don't think.'

The doctor and I had nothing in common. Our
conversations were stilted and painfully contrived. I
don't remember what we talked about. His work, I
suppose; my father's health. I recall asking him about
books but he had no time to read, and when I told KK
this, she told me I should have stopped it right there.
I complained to my mother, moaned about the awk-
wardness of his phone calls. 'But these things take time,'
my mother said with determined hope, though I understood it was best if we didn't take too much time. 'Love
comes after marriage,' she reminded me.

His mother called mine often, rekindling the
friendship from their university days. We skipped the
hospital one afternoon and drove down the M1 to their
house for lunch. I met his sisters but I barely spoke
to him at all. His family came to my eldest brother's
wedding which took place on a hot August afternoon,
my father allowed out from hospital in his wheelchair,
and the doctor and I smiled and skirted around each

other, while I felt his mother watching the way I moved around the venue. Our conversations continued on the phone, polite but dull. Then, after a few slow months of this dragging on, as painful as a toothache with no end in sight, I received a text in which he apologised in a confused and vague way and said that there was someone else but he'd not yet told his mum so please could I not tell mine, and then it all just fizzled away. My mother never heard from his mother again.

I have this terrible feeling that if the doctor had agreed to marry me I might have gone along with it because that was what I was supposed to do. Just so it would have been over, dusted, done.

THESE DAYS

'WHAT WOULD YOU DO WITHOUT ME?' Sina flings his arms around me and shouts down my ear, just as I'm trying to sneak a little work in on my laptop at the dining table.

'Honestly, I think I'd have a nice long sleep,' I say,

kissing his cheek but also trying to shift my laptop out of his way. 'Or I'd get a lot of writing done.'

A deadpan 'Very funny, Mama' comes from the floor, where Suffian is building something complicated from Lego. He doesn't look up.

'YOU WILL SLEEP AND I WILL WAKE YOU!' Sina says, beaming at me with a determination that is almost frightening. Jude is also trying to join in. He is holding my legs, attempting to push Sina out of the way.

With a sigh, I put my laptop away. As I do, Suffian pipes up from his heap on the floor again. 'Anyway, Mama, *I* don't know what I'd do without you . . .'

'Oh, Suffi! Me neither!'

'. . . But one day you will die. Because everyone does. Even spiders. Even rabbits! Die. Die, die, die.'

THOSE DAYS

After the doctor disappeared, life resumed. Months passed, rolling on. Nothing much changed. My dad stayed in the hospital for nearly two years. It felt endless. The doctors never talked about him being discharged but they never talked about what would happen if he wasn't either. Sometimes the left side of his body curled up tight, stiff like a dead leaf, and we had to massage his limbs to release the tension and all I could feel was the sharpness of his hollow bones that felt as though they might snap. Seeing him like this was the worst thing in my life. Was this really what God wanted for him?

Everyone who wasn't living it said that my dad's illness and what was left of his life was God's will, Allah ki marzi. They said it sadly, as though there was nothing we could do about it, because we weren't supposed to question God's ways. Alone, I wondered why God would want to do this to him, to anyone. I begged God to be kinder. I couldn't understand why any of this had happened to my dad, why any of it was happening to us.

Sometimes, mostly in the quiet shadows of a dark, starless night, I allowed myself to consider what God might have wanted for me, if God was even thinking of me. I could do nothing to help my dad. But I wondered if I might do something to help myself. This was the year I would turn twenty-five, which at the time felt like a significant milestone. It struck me that it was urgent to have some sort of a plan in place. One night after another long day at the hospital, I stayed up late in my room in the glow of my laptop and guiltily, hungrily, applied for a position at the *Observer* in London.

I didn't think I'd stand a chance but somehow I did and I got it. For just a moment, I felt a small thrill of excitement and pride, but then a dark, cavernous guilt swallowed me whole. With my brothers away in London, most of the day-to-day hospital caring fell to my mother and me, and while she was at work, it was my responsibility. I knew she depended on me. My mother was so worried and it seemed as though she might shrink under the weight of it all and disappear. It broke my heart to watch her try to be so brave and the thought of leaving my dad destroyed me, but at the same time something was tugging at me like a premonition. I knew I had to take the job, even though the thought of leaving was tearing me to bits.

I told her. She listened.

'Take it,' she said. 'It's a big opportunity. We didn't send you to all those schools and universities just to do nothing, to sit in the hospital all day. We'll be okay. You've done so well to get it. You must go, and make the most of it.'

My chest hurt; everything felt so heavy. I had dreaded her reaction but she had responded with only kindness. I felt so ashamed to have expected the worst but more than that I felt the weight of her love fall into me as she kissed my cheek, my eyes tingling with tears.

I wanted to tell my dad but I wasn't sure he would understand. When he first lost his speech, we gave him notebooks and pens to see if he could write to us instead. His scribbles were shaky and confusing, odd observations written in his doctor's sprawl. When he wrote about me, it was as though he saw me locked in the past, still a schoolgirl with white socks pulled up to my knees. I took his hand and I told him that I was grown now and had a new job. I told him I hoped he'd be proud, even if it was the *Observer* (he was more of a *Sunday Times* man). 'I'm not leaving you,' I said. 'It's just I think I have to give this a go. Is that okay?'

He stared into my eyes and blinked twice for yes as we pressed our foreheads together in silence.

Weeks later, just as I was about to start at the *Observer*, my father was moved to another hospital. It was a high-rise and all you could see through the window was the scaffolding of the sky, the clouds moving slowly by. One morning, on a particularly bright but chilly spring day, the sunlight slanted through the window, briefly illuminating a constellation of dust motes turning in the corner. For a moment the whole room glowed like honey and then, just like that, my father died.

THESE DAYS

It still gets me, the sadness. It comes at odd moments, often when I least expect it, and sometimes it is so faint I can't quite put a name to it. I have come to understand that it will always be there, a shadow or a summer breeze. Over the years, my grief has softened into a simple sort of sadness. I have stopped overthinking it. I miss him, that is all.

I struggle to remember sometimes how long it's been. Though I know he died in March, my mind cannot automatically remember the date. I could not tell you off the top of my head what year he died; I'd have to work it out, count backwards on my fingers and then forwards again. I suppose I am protecting myself from something. But I will always remember what it felt like, to feel him slip away. I will always remember the emptiness.

There will come a point in the future where my father will have been dead for half of my life. I imagine the fact of this will hit me hard, when that time comes, when I realise how much he's missed out on. Or perhaps it won't. Maybe I'll find a way to let the shadow pass, to sit in the breeze and think of all the good things.

Jude and I do this thing when we look for the moon every night before he goes to sleep. Sometimes when we look out at the velvet night sky and the dark shifting clouds, for just a second the immensity of it, of space and the overspilling universe, catches in my throat and I think: where is he, can he see me now, does he remember who I am? Sometimes I find myself looking for him on the bus or the Tube. Every summer, I half expect to find him in the garden centre smelling of the earth and the air and the outdoors, the way he always smelt on Sunday, after mowing the lawn in his vest with a handkerchief knotted around his head. Sometimes I wonder what I'd do if I saw him again. If he'd even recognise me.

There are times when my heart tricks me into allowing myself to wonder, just for a moment, what my life would be like if he was still in it. I try not to play that game too much. I talk about him to my children in cheerful ways, as though he were a character in one of their books. They find it funny that he had a moustache because 'Nobody has a moustache!' I tell them how he jingled his car keys and how he once bought me a lemon-yellow bike with a white basket and it was the most amazing bike I'd ever seen. I tell them that he'd have built them a treehouse; they tell me it's too bad he's dead, because they'd really, really like a treehouse. I tell them he'd have loved them very, very much.

In the beginning, it mattered to me to have something that belonged to him. For a long time, I kept a bottle of his Ralph Lauren aftershave I'd swiped from his hospital toiletries bag and a jolly, bright red V-neck jumper from French Connection that I'd always thought made him look so cheery. I kept them towards the front of my wardrobe, just so that they'd be there, touchable, as I reached for a top or a bottle of lotion of my own, but eventually they were lost in the jumble of my clothes and pushed, unknowingly, to the back. I found them when I was clearing out my flat, and preparing to move in with Richard. By then, the aftershave smelt like vinegar, the jumper old and unfamiliar. I poured the stale aftershave down the sink, the jumper went to charity. They came nowhere close to representing the sum of him, of who he was. They were just things.

On New Year's Eve a few years ago, Richard and I were watching a movie when all of a sudden I was overcome and it had nothing to do with the film.

'Hey,' Richard said. 'What's wrong?'

It had just hit me, that was all, that another year had gone and I said in a quiet voice: 'It's been so long. So, so long.' And though I didn't say much more then, and though Richard had never met my father, he knew what I was trying to say. He pulled me to him and I felt understood, somehow.

When we were first engaged, someone asked me if I thought my father would have approved. The way the question was posed, it was clear the person asking thought the answer was no. Honestly, I don't know what my father's immediate knee-jerk reaction might have been if he'd been well. I'm sure he would have had concerns. I think he'd have heard me out, the way he heard me out about all the other things I'd ever wanted to do. I think he'd have come around and set the tone. But I can't change the past. He did have that awful stroke. Even if he had survived, I suppose the best I could have hoped for is that he might have understood and blinked twice for yes, his forehead pressed to mine.

EARLY MARCH, 2011

After our tea at Tinderbox, Richard messages me the very same night. He says he'd like to see me again soon and suggests dinner in a couple of days if

I am free. I look at my phone and my heart sinks, not because I don't want to see him but because I really, really do.

I stop and wonder what my mother would think. Then I remind myself that it's just dinner, just one dinner for God's sake, and that especially after everything that happened with that guy from the matrimonial agency, I deserve this much at least. I remind myself that I have every right to do this.

So we go for dinner, a Thai place in Old Street, and though the restaurant is packed and noisy, when I look at him and when we talk, I feel as though we are the only two people there. I can't explain it to myself in any rational way, only that it feels both intense and natural, only that it hasn't ever felt like this with any of the so-called suitable boys I have met before.

Later I am offered press tickets for a film festival. I ask Richard if he'd like to come with me. London has been rioting all day against government cuts and there are thousands of angry people in the streets. Police vans screech past and pull to a halt. Officers jump out into the road. The police are kettling the protestors and as we try to make our way across Piccadilly right in front of the picket line, he takes my hand for the first time and I let him hold it and lead the way.

The film festival is a small independent one, and I know nothing about the film we are watching because I didn't read the press release. It turns out that the film is about an Indian-American boy in his twenties whose parents are quite strict and then he falls for an American girl and doesn't know what to do. As the plot painfully unfolds, I shift in my seat. I am mortified and I cringe in the dark, hoping desperately that he doesn't see this as some giant, tactless hint because I really did not intend for it to be. At some point, I let go of his hand and I am sad when he doesn't reach for it back. When the film is over, he looks at me quizzically, curious.

On the days we don't see each other, we talk on the phone and message throughout the day. He tells me small, incidental things about his life, his family, the farm where he grew up, but none of it feels like small talk and the familiarity of all of it begins to stitch us together. I tell him about my dad, my writing, the meaning of my name. Sometimes I send him links to pieces I've done and he sends me playlists and we talk about what's going on in the world. I feel, for the first time, as though there is no rush.

THOSE DAYS

I postponed starting my job at the *Observer* until a fortnight after my father's funeral. I felt terrible about leaving my mum but I also knew I'd be back most weekends and I tried to hold on to that. 'I'll call you every day,' I said as I left, and I meant it; I wanted to. I cried most of the two-and a-half-hour drive to my brother's place, where I was to sleep on his sofa temporarily (I couldn't afford to rent anywhere on my tiny salary).

On my first day at the *Observer*, an editorial assistant from one of the lifestyle sections came down to collect me from reception nearly an hour later than I'd been told to be there. 'Don't take it personally if we forget that you're here!' she said, all flickety-flick with her hair. 'We're not being rude, it's just we're very, very busy! You'll have to figure a lot out yourself!' The arrangement suited me because I wasn't especially in the mood for small talk. I wasn't sure who, apart from my immediate desk editor, knew that my dad had died because I didn't mention it and nobody asked.

Sometimes I had an urge to get away from my desk and I'd push my chair back and rush to the stairwell, running up a level so no one from my floor would see me. I stood there, looking out the window at the busy street and the moving traffic and the tiny people below, trying to steady myself. Lately I had noticed my fingers had started to tremble when I typed and that my throat swelled for no reason, as though a chunk of dry bread was stuck in it.

KK and my other university friends tried to keep me busy. We had weekly dinners at Carluccio's, which seemed grown-up at the time, but I felt as though I was only half there and, honestly, at times I dreaded seeing them. I was irrationally jealous because they had dads with beating hearts who called them on their birthdays and reminded them to open savings accounts and I didn't. I think my friends thought the way to make me feel better was to keep me busy and distracted; to talk about anything but my dad in order to keep my mind off him. I knew they were trying to help and I didn't want to seem ungrateful, but I found the effort involved in meeting up after work and trying not to cry exhausting, and pretending things were normal only made me feel worse. Back in Walsall, in the immediate aftermath of my dad's death, our house filled with family friends and relatives who brought huge pots of biryani and made endless cups of tea and stacked up slim individual chapters of the Quran for visitors to read silently while I recounted the moment he passed away to those who asked, because they did ask, because they wanted to know. And though it was at times draining to go over it, again and again, it also felt necessary. It felt important not to forget.

But in London, in a new job, in a new city, sleeping on my brother's sofa, there was nothing to root me to all of that. I didn't have aunties filling up the fridge with food or taking me into their arms or blessing me with prayers and promising me that God would give me takat, strength. Living with my brother gave me some comfort and familiarity, but I still felt very much on my own in some ways, because though we could talk about the sequence of events that led to our father's death, we didn't, or couldn't, articulate how it made us feel on the inside. We'd never had to do it before.

I was lonely but I also knew that I couldn't possibly be as lonely as my mum, and this made my heart so heavy, it hurt even more. I didn't know where I was supposed to be – in the city, trying to be a journalist, though I hardly had the courage to speak, or back home in Walsall, with my mum. Everything was blurred. It felt as though the prescription for my contact lenses was wrong because things looked slightly different, a touch off-kilter. I even had my eyes tested but they were fine. The thing that had changed was something deeper inside me. I joined the gym as an excuse to skip those weekly dinners with my university friends, because though I knew they meant well, I couldn't face sitting in a restaurant eating pasta like a normal person, when my father was not long dead. I needed space, even from friends, even from KK, and so I built a small wall around me and started going to the gym almost every day to avoid socialising. There, I discovered that running on the treadmill until my heart pounded and I could barely breathe was one way of not having to think.

Other times, my sadness followed so closely in my footsteps I couldn't outrun it. Once I saw an older man on the Tube who bore a strong resemblance to my dad from before he got sick. His glasses, the side-parting in his fine nut-brown hair. The likeness startled me and I stared. The man caught me looking at him and smiled politely, and I couldn't bear it. I got off the Tube at the next stop even though it wasn't mine, sobbing messy tears, gasping in between for breath.

At some point I went to the GP for something unrelated and when I started crying, he told me what I was feeling was normal and one of the stages of grief.

'Do you have someone you can talk to?' the doctor said.

'Sort of,' I said, sniffing. I wonder what he would have done if I had told him the truth, which was that though there were people in my life, I was so frightened of what I was feeling I couldn't show it to them in case it scared them away. The emptiness sat inside me, surrounded me. I grew frightened of the dark; at night I slept with a lamp on, like a little girl. I slept a lot during this time, deep and heavy, and still woke up exhausted. I didn't remember what I dreamed of. It was all just a blank.

I couldn't seem to make sense of the simplest of things. My birthday came and went, and like a child I sat cross-legged on the floor trying to come to terms with the most basic fact that my dad would never again pick up a pen with his fingers and sign a card for me, because he was gone and didn't exist any more. It made no sense. For so long, my life and my family's life had revolved around the hospital and though it wasn't a pleasant place to be, it formed a sort of bubble around us. I had been desperate to leave the hospital and its staleness behind but now that we had, I felt strangely unanchored and, in an odd way, I missed it. Months later, I found myself back there, bearing Christmas gifts for staff and long-term patients we had come to know in a roundabout way. But just walking down the corridor that led to his ward was too much and I left the presents on the floor and ran out of the hospital, falling to the pavement in a crying heap. Because of course it wasn't the hospital I missed. It was always my dad, and I'd been missing him for a long time already.

The world felt muffled, as though I was under water, and I was frequently startled by the most normal of things: a doorbell, the vibration of a text message, my boss calling my name to bring my attention back from the vast spaces it tended to wander off to. I walked in this strange fog of bewilderment, detached from the world, wondering if I'd ever fully be a part of it again.

When my dad died that bright morning in March, I was by his bedside along with one of my brothers. My mum had stepped out of the room to pray and in those few minutes he took his last breaths, ragged and hoarse. Hours later, I sat in the front of an ambulance taking him from the hospital to the mosque; the driver took several corners too fast and I was startled by the hollow, heavy thuds of his body rattling in the back. Inside, I was raging. I wanted to scream at the driver to slow down; didn't he know that was my dad back there? But instead I said nothing. I looked out of the window and sat in silence, tears running down my face.

There is nothing that can possibly make seeing someone you love die any easier. Even now, I can't get my head around how someone can be alive one minute, alive for years and years with a heart that beats full of feelings and a mind full of thoughts and a life that is so loved, and then dead the next. Gone, in the second it takes for a fleck of dust to turn and settle in a corner of a room. Of all the things I was scared of, it was this that kept me up late at night and made it so hard to breathe: knowing that it would eventually happen to all the people I loved. Knowing that I would be left again and again, until it happened to me too.

MID TO LATE MARCH, 2011

Soon after the film festival, Richard and I arrange to go for dinner in Hampstead. The restaurant is halal (I choose it for this reason; neither of us are vegetarian yet). At another table, an elderly-looking man is browsing the menu but when he discovers the halal disclaimer, he gets cross and shouts at the waitress. He is Jewish, he shouts, and he will not stand for this! He leaves without ordering. A few moments later, Richard says: 'What would it mean for your family, if they were to know, if we were to be together?'

I stare down at the table and in that moment it's as if I suddenly wake up.

My family doesn't know about us; of course they don't. I still call my mother every day, though lately our conversations have been difficult and I can't always think of what to say. Right now, she thinks I'm with KK.

This won't mean anything for my family, because it can't. We can't be together; it's not even up for debate. All my upbringing has been to stop something like this happening. I feel a sensation similar to tripping up over a kerb and I realise that whatever I have been trying to pretend that this is, it has to end before it has even started, before there are too many lies, before it is too hard to walk away. I look at him. There is something about him that is so steady, so sincere. All I want is for him to pull me to him, let me lay my head upon his chest (he doesn't; I don't). The way he looks at me reminds me I can tell him anything. I take a deep breath and I try to explain.

I tell him in a small voice that we can't be together because my religion won't allow it and my family won't either. I smile brightly, tell him I'm sorry I have wasted his time. He covers my hand with his.

'We really can't be together? Like, at all?' he says. He tells me he's been reading up on it; I wonder what he's been googling.

'Well, sure we could,' I say coolly. 'You could convert and marry me but that's never going to happen. I'm not even supposed to date. I'm sorry, I shouldn't really be here. I shouldn't have even . . .' I remove my hand, gesture in his direction. I sigh in an ugly way that sounds mean and twisted coming out of my mouth.

The strange thing is he doesn't bat an eyelid.

'Yeah, that's what I'd read. About converting. I've been reading up on Islam, as it happens. A lot of similarities, as far as I can see.' His face is entirely serious.

I laugh, even though it's not remotely funny. I tell him again, once more, that our being together is out of the question, just to be sure he understands.

'I gave up drinking a while ago!' he says in an optimistic way, trying to lighten the mood. I smile weakly because though I had already noticed that he didn't drink, I also know it is nowhere near enough.

We eat dinner quietly. We leave. We walk in silence down the steep Hampstead streets. I don't know what to do with my hands. I consider that this will probably be the last time I see him.

But the problem is something has already started, even though I am not sure what it is. We are inching closer to each other without fully understanding it. Every day my head is full of him. Though my self-belief has been run down to the ground by the rejections I have received over the last seven years and by the disappointment and the weariness and the sadness and the grief and the ugly feeling that I am not good enough to be loved, I am struck by an unusual sense of certainty that he cares about me. Something is there, between us. Now I must let it go. We walk down the hill, hands stuffed in our pockets, past the elegant white houses, and I feel as though I might cry. There it is, the familiar sensation of being so close but so far, stepping away from the edge of something that would now happen to somebody else.

It is the night of the supermoon, the biggest and brightest moon in nearly two decades. The hilly streets of Hampstead are crowded. Everyone is gazing up in awe, waving their phones in the air like flickering candles. The night sky is as dark and glossy as black coffee and then I see it too, the moon rolling towards us between the rooftops like a beachball, bright as a giant light bulb. I look down at my shoes. In the moonlight, even the asphalt glows. He stops and puts a hand on my arm.

'Hey,' he says. 'Come here.'

THESE DAYS

For Christmas, Richard's parents gift us a weekend away and offer to look after the kids. It is the first time we have ever gone away for a night, just the two of us, excluding the times I've gone into labour, which don't exactly count.

Other couples we know have regular date nights and leave their children with babysitters or grand-parents, but we've never got around to this. We've had a few rare evenings out together over the years, a din-ner, a movie, but nothing regular. His parents and my mother live too far away and we never got around to finding a local babysitter. For the longest time, leav-ing the boys has seemed impossible, all too young, too many of them, too unpredictable to leave in someone else's hands.

'Do you think they'll be okay?' I ask him. Inevitably, in the run-up to this weekend, Jude has decided he does not want to sleep and has been waking up frequently in the middle of the night. I am worried that if he wakes up in the night and neither of us are there, he won't settle.

'The boys or my parents?'

I think for a minute. 'All of them,' I say.

'Oh well, they'll have to be. It's out of our hands once we leave!' he says.

We arrive at a smart townhouse hotel in Chiswick. Richard has been unusually quiet on the way and I wonder if we have turned into one of those couples, the ones who don't have anything to say to each other without their children around them to punctuate their time and centre their conversations. When we are in our room, I ask him if he's okay. I don't want us to be one of those couples.

'You're being quiet.'

'Am I?'

'Yeah.'

'Oh.'

'Do you think we're turning into one of those couples, the ones who don't have anything to say to each other without their children around?'

He looks at me and laughs.

'No. I don't think that at all.'

'Then how come you're being so quiet?'

'Because I didn't realise how knackered I am.'

'Okay, then.'

'Okay, then.'

He comes over to where I am standing and touches my face with his hand and smiles. 'I'm fine, honestly,' he says and then I stop worrying.

The hotel is tastefully luxurious. It's unusual, being able to talk and eat without the constant interruption and we only check our phones a few times to make sure the boys are in bed. The next day, neither of us particularly wants to leave. We take a walk down to the river, hand in hand, and I catch sight of our reflection and say: 'Do you think we look old or young?' and he says young, definitely young, but we both know we are starting to look closer to middle-aged. We walk slowly, wondering how late we can get away with being. I tell Richard that I have missed the boys but I have also missed us, this.

'I know what you mean,' he says and though we have been married for so long now, as comfortable as old socks and Sunday roasts, I still feel the rush of love as he leans in towards me. When we get home, the kids barely notice us and though we are slightly miffed by this, we both agree that it is in general a good thing.

THOSE DAYS

After sleeping on my brother's sofa, I moved in with my friend Suzanne from university, whose parents had bought her a little terraced house in East London near the docks. It had a tiny front room with a bright blue sofa, a long and sunlit kitchen overlooking a patch of grass, and two tidy bedrooms. Her spare room was a haven for friends who needed a place to stay but couldn't afford London rents: she refused to charge anything like the going rate. Though the house was sweet, welcoming and warm, the girls who moved in and out before me never stayed too long. Everyone had arrived in London with hopes of big-city living but back then, this corner of East London lay half asleep in the long shadow of Canary Wharf. There was a Costcutter further up towards the dock and a petrol station across the road, but not much more than that. The DLR didn't fully exist yet: getting to the nearest station meant climbing two tall stairwells, crossing a high bridge over the water, and then a further walk past the Excel Centre. One by one, the girls before me had moved into one-bed flats with their boyfriends or, if there was no boyfriend, into a house-share somewhere more central where they were more likely to meet someone who might eventually become a boyfriend. They moved to places like Hoxton and Pimlico, Shoreditch and Angel, parts of town with places to go and things to do, places where the air didn't hang heavy with a curious blend of contrasting smells from the Beckton Sewage Treatment Works and the Tate & Lyle refinery down by the Thames. I lived there for three years. I call them the Sad Girl Years.

Suzanne was what my mother would have called a sensible, good girl. She had a first in law and a brilliantly paid job at a top law firm. She also had a long-term boyfriend, Mark; they had been together since the start of university. Suzanne was lovely. Mark was also lovely. They lived a calm, grown-up existence full of good, solid life choices. On the rare evenings that they were not working late, they would cook together, watch *Question Time* or organise their finances. I microwaved baked potatoes, went to work in my jeans, and earned less in a year on the newspaper than Suzanne made in a quarter; Suzanne wore suits, worked long, hard hours and still batch-cooked on Sundays. Although Suzanne and Mark were friendly and kind and never seemed to mind me being around, I felt acutely aware of being a child in their presence, a third wheel living in what should have been the nursery, so far behind them in every way.

Over the three years that I lived with Suzanne, I began to long for what she had with Mark (not *him*, I hasten to add: what they had). I wanted to give someone a key, to come home from work to them waiting for me, to watch something on TV with their arm around me. I longed to feel this comfort, the steadiness of warmth and affection. I wondered what it was like to be loved and cared for by someone who had found you, someone who was meant for you. To walk in the world every day with such certainty.

⌒

Of course, I was aware that there was more to life than simply being with someone. I'd been at the *Observer* for three years and I had grown in confidence, even if I was still at times painfully shy around my colleagues. It still thrilled me to know that my articles were being read. Important people were noticing me; I had even won awards. I was finding opportunities, pitching to other parts of the paper, writing stories about things that mattered to me. Editors from other publications began to contact me, asking if I was interested in writing for them, because they had read my work. My desk editor brought her neighbour's daughter into work with her for a week of work experience, sitting her next to me and handing her bylines on a plate as though they were biscuits for the taking. Every now and then I had to shake myself to remember that I was there, in the middle of the newsroom, through doors I had somehow managed to open on my own without the luck of well-connected, well-heeled neighbours in high places.

But work alone was not enough: I still had this hole of emptiness and I was certain only somebody else could fill it. I didn't realise then that this was unhealthy, that the void was something I needed to deal with myself. I had no experience of the sort of confidence that celebrated being single, that insisted there was no shame or embarrassment in it, that there was no hurry. I didn't believe that it was possible for me to feel that way.

I tried to think about things other than being married or not married. KK told me about vision boards and convinced me to have a go. We sat on the floor with a stack of magazines, cross-legged with glue sticks and blank pieces of card as though we were children doing crafts, listening to John Mayer because that's what we did back then. Her board was full of pictures of book covers and writing retreats and quiet rooms with a view where she might write her novel. My board had a picture of a house, a garden, a handsome stock-photo man, and an engagement ring. 'Oh,' KK said.

Some mornings before work, waking up with an ache I couldn't put a name to, I gave myself silent pep talks in bed or facing the mirror. 'Get over yourself,' I'd say, rolling my eyes at my reflection, reminding myself I was incredibly lucky to have landed a job on a national newspaper, reciting the line from *The Devil Wears Prada* that a million others would kill for it (something my desk editor occasionally reminded me of, with a raise of her eyebrow and a cluck of her tongue whenever she caught me lost in my head again; 'Maybe not a million,' I'd say). I tried to focus, find work that was meaningful, write things that mattered, but I still couldn't shake the feeling that it didn't matter what words came out of my mouth, what opinions I held in my head or wrote in print. My individual achievements would never matter as much as being married. I felt this, even though my parents were incredibly proud of everything I'd done academically and professionally; for the longest time, my mother covered the fridge door with my articles until she realised there were too many to collect and the novelty understandably wore off. But I'd always felt, underneath, that marriage trumped everything. My parents never said this explicitly, but I somehow absorbed it in the way I saw the lives of so many girls and cousins unfold around me, engaged before they'd finished their medical degrees, married by the age of twenty-three, living with their in-laws and new families. There was so much that was unsaid, and so much that felt expected.

I was now twenty-seven, already considered old (a fact various relatives liked to remind me of), and the number of people approaching my mother with proposals or interest had reduced. Aunties and married women my own age looked me up and down at dinner parties and other people's weddings as though I was a tragedy; there were barbed questions and snarky comments about my appearance. Sometimes people still brought up my short time in Paris as a sign of my apparent waywardness, elaborating on the myth of the dreamy French boy who had whisked me away to do a master's degree. I felt scrutinised like cut glass, held up to the light for dust or smudged fingerprints. I was aware that some of the girls I'd grown up with found me aloof because I'd moved away; I'd overheard it said that I came across as arrogant, and my mum frequently reminded me to make more of an effort. But I never thought I was better than anyone; the truth was, I didn't think much of myself.

I hated that so many people from my world measured a woman's worth by her appearance, the lightness of her skin, the slimness of her waist, her marriageability, and I hated that this was how it had to be because I knew we were so much more, that I was so much more than that, but I was also tired of feeling lonely. Sometimes I found myself crying for no apparent reason, on the treadmill, on the bus, my hand reaching up to my damp face as though it was someone else's, brushing away tears that did not seem to stop.

~

In the years after my father's death, I felt awkward in my own skin in a way that was more pronounced than it ever had been before. Sometimes I couldn't even bring myself to eat lunch with colleagues, finding excuses to avoid talking too much, which, as a journalist, sometimes made my job awkward. From the moment I sat down at my desk each morning, I felt nervous, fearful of messing up or being caught out for making a mistake, and this became exhausting over time. At work dos I frequently felt as though I was looking in from the outside, a moth batting against a window before falling away. Sometimes this suited me, because I wasn't very good at socialising anyway and I often felt out of place at media parties when everyone else was drinking, but there was a big difference between being wilfully alone and being lonely.

One of my good university friends had recently moved to New York, to be with a man she met in Sainsbury's in Highbury. She'd dropped something, he'd picked it up, he found her at the checkout and that was that. It all happened so fast, but it was love, she said, and the rest of us marvelled at her luck. And like a terrible bitter sort of friend, I also felt more than a little jealous. Because I wanted a love story too. I wanted a meet-cute, I wanted romance. It was the only thing, I was sure, that would distract me from the emptiness and stop me feeling sad. 'What are the odds,' I said to KK, 'of something like that happening to us?'

'Honestly? Slim to none,' she said, matter-of-fact.

She was right. The probability of me meeting a suitable boy who just so happened to share my background and my family values by chance was especially unlikely, considering all the criteria I needed to fulfil. I realised that if I didn't want to be lonely any more, I needed help. I needed to do things the way they had always been done. And so, on a weekend visit home, I

awkwardly mumbled to my mother that I was ready
to be introduced again to suitors and she was, I think,
delighted because she didn't have to coax me into it
herself. I began to resign myself to the idea of having
someone chosen for me, and at first this left me with
a sinking feeling. Of course, my mum would never
have made me marry someone I didn't want to – it
was never about that; it was that in my heart, I yearned
for romance and in my mind, unfairly perhaps, I felt
that wouldn't be possible if my mother and his mother
were involved from the outset.

Ever since I was twelve, and my English teacher
first handed me a copy of Georgette Heyer's *Friday's
Child*, I'd dreamed of an incredibly romantic love,
and though it may sound naive, that was a big part
of why I resisted my parents all those years ago in
Italy. I didn't know then how I would find love but
I believed I would, somehow. Now, I wasn't so sure.
I told myself to stop being childish; so many people I
knew had been introduced to each other by their parents in the so-called traditional way. It worked for them
and they were happy and in love – or at least that's what

it looked like. All I had to do was look right in front of me: my own parents had been introduced as rishtas, my mother's older brother suggesting the match, and they still had the sweetest romance, a deep love, a profound connection. They held hands during evening walks around the block that they were always trying to get me to go on and left each other Post-it notes on the inside of their wardrobe door saying *Love you heaps!* and called each other Jaan, darling. More than that, they moved in harmony together. They knew what the other was thinking, finished each other's sentences; always a united front. I remembered what my mother told me, that love comes after marriage. I began to consider the possibility that this could be a good thing.

'Maybe it won't be so bad,' I told KK. 'I guess it's easier to be with someone who's been vetted, someone you don't have to explain everything about the way your family does things to, because their family's more or less the same. I thought that didn't matter before, but it does. I can understand that now.'

KK's mother was also starting to worry about her daughter being single, suggesting nice Nigerian men for her to meet, but KK was able to laugh about it whereas I'd lost my humour some time ago.

'You mean like . . . explaining the water bottle?' The water bottle was something I had kept hidden in the bathroom of our shared student house and still kept hidden in Suzanne's house, though everyone was aware of its existence. Muslims are taught to use water to wash instead of just dry loo roll.

'Oh do piss off, please,' I said.

THESE DAYS

My brothers will often, for reasons best left unwritten, discuss various forms of the water bottle, more commonly known as a lota, when sitting around the dining table after dinner. It makes my mother despair. In short, most of my cousins and my sisters-in-law find it hilarious that my brothers and I were taught to manoeuvre it from behind, whereas apparently most people do it from the front. I don't want to get into the logistics; it is neither appropriate nor relevant. Richard, who like most, if not all, English people was not taught to use a lota, listens to these conversations highly bemused.

When one of my brothers learned about Richard, he sent me a number of angry emails in which he said: *I just don't see this happening. I cannot approve. He'll simply not fit in with our family. I cannot even imagine having a conversation with him at the dining table.*

To date, Richard has sat around the dining table and listened to my family's toilet hygiene habits for almost a decade. Honestly, I think we're good.

THOSE DAYS

And so, the matchmaking was renewed once again, in earnest. I was aware that now that I was a few years off thirty I wouldn't be most prospective families' first choice. A good friend of mine from Walsall, Salma Baji, who was like an older sister to me, raked through her phone contacts to find someone she thought might be eligible. The problem was, all the potentially eligible

South Asian people she knew were doctors or dentists, like their fathers, and sometimes their mothers. For some reason, perhaps to do with mortgages or perhaps because they were passionate about their jobs, these doctors and dentists only wanted to marry other doctors and dentists. On this basis alone, I was a wildcard, automatically eliminated from the pool.

Once Salma Baji put me in touch with someone who was, she told me excitedly, 'creative like you! He's in fashion!' It turned out he was designing football slogans to print on Fruit of the Loom T-shirts from his teenage bedroom and then trying to sell them online. He was ten years older than me. He was very excited about his plans, and as much as I was (and am) all for anyone following their dreams and doing things differently, I couldn't quite muster the same enthusiasm.

An aunty from America called my mother with details of her forty-year-old nephew, who had moved to London from Lahore. I had met her family on holiday once; her daughters were both stunningly beautiful and married by twenty-one and my mother thought they were angels; I was certain she wished I was more like them. I met him in Starbucks in Covent Garden and though he was keen, I couldn't get past the horrifying fact that he looked a little bit like Saddam Hussein in a lemon V-neck sweater. He rushed to tell me I was prettier than he thought I would be, given how old I was, and then, as though it were an afterthought, he mentioned he needed an extension on his visa and oh, could I help?

Every few weeks, my contact details were passed along through a chain of aunties to reach someone in Berkshire or Milton Keynes, and I'd receive a text or an email and maybe sometimes even a call, but then I'd run out of things to talk or text about because, well, what was I supposed to say? It was like the doctor up the M1 all over again. Often, their parents gave my mother 'feedback' based on their sons' assessment of me, which was that they were looking for 'a more traditional, homely girl'. My mother called me and asked me what on earth I was saying to them to put them all off. I got more critical feedback through aunties than I ever did in my annual appraisals at work, though it was not exactly helpful for my personal self-development.

I thought that perhaps I was more likely to find someone myself through a Muslim-specific singles site. I'd seen one advertised on the Tube. I told my mother about it and, wearily, she conceded it was worth a try. KK proofread my profile and up it went. I trawled through profiles of men detailing their hunt for 'family girls' who were 'not too Western' and 'not too educated' in the hope I'd find someone I might be inclined to meet. I tried to be positive and proactive even though I didn't feel like it. But in this strange world of chaste halal dating, where you size up a potential spouse in the time it takes to order a decaf, I realised quite quickly that it didn't matter who I was; it was *what* I was that mattered more.

I could be anyone, I remember thinking over endless polite coffees on halal dates with strangers in public places on damp, cold evenings when all I wanted to do was go home and lock the door. I could be anyone, I thought on the way home, as I ended up deleting yet another number from my phone. I could be anyone, as long as I was a good Muslim woman who was not too complicated and didn't want too much.

Once I found someone on the Muslim website whom I recognised from a literary event. 'Could this be it?!' I thought. I sent his profile to KK and she emailed back a chain of exclamation marks because, yeah, there was something about him. His profile mentioned a love of Chekhov's short stories and a guilty pleasure for watching old episodes of *Party of Five* on Channel Four, both things I could wholeheartedly appreciate. It turned out he lived in Edgbaston with his family; I wrote back, upbeat, telling him that I had gone to school in Edgbaston and so on, thinking it might be some small-world coincidence to connect us, but he stopped things short. He was appalled, disgusted even, to hear that I didn't live with my mother in Walsall and took my choice to live alone and work in London to mean that I had put myself first. His older brother's wife had already moved in and he expected his own wife to do the same.

To be honest, I find it incredibly selfish how so many young Asians seem to forget their cultural and family struc-ture, he wrote to me. He went on to tell me that my values were misplaced, my sense of duty lost. I was far too Western for him, he said. He wanted a wife who understood her sense of responsibility, not someone like me who'd left her widowed mother living on her own. I felt as though I'd been spat on by a stranger and it shook me up so much, I deleted my profile.

There was one person who seemed like he might be a real, tangible possibility. His parents and mine were family friends. We'd grown up circling each other at weekend dinner parties; he had come to my house countless times but, like most of those boys, I'd never talked to him. All I knew about him was what I'd heard in roundabout ways – that he was very clever, that he lived in London, that he liked cricket. It helped that as a teenager I had admired his indie-band looks. My mum phoned me one evening to tell me that she had heard from a trustworthy aunty, who was good friends with both his mother and mine, that his mother had asked about me. My mum's voice was nervous – this was in theory a good match, a very good match, in terms of each other's backgrounds and families. It occurred to me that if I married him, life would theoretically be easy: our families knew all the same people, attended all the same social gatherings and even though I rarely enjoyed these things, I thought of what a relief it would be not to have to break into a brand new Pakistani social scene as somebody's wife. My mind worked quickly – he worked in London so I wouldn't have to try and find a new job somewhere else or relocate (it was almost always on the bride to do this, if the groom lived elsewhere) or move in with his parents. Though they weren't necessarily best friends, my brothers were friendly with him and this, I thought, was a good sign.

I told Salma Baji, who had already heard of his family's interest along the grapevine, and she agreed – this would be a wonderful thing. It didn't matter that I'd barely said anything to him in all the years I'd known him, or rather known of him. I decided to make an effort. I returned to the Walsall dinner parties and looked out for him, my teenage crush rekindled. I made sure to greet his mother enthusiastically or to talk to his sister-in-law.

His family's assessment of me went on for many months. I kept asking my mum if she'd heard anything, or if they'd said anything specific, but all she knew from the aunty who was acting as the go-between was that they were thinking about it. I didn't know if the 'they' included the boy, or just his parents. She told me to be patient. So I kept driving home for other people's weddings and dinners, kept trying to be more visible to him and his family, making more of an effort with my make-up or choosing a more elaborate shalwar kameez in a bid to seem refined or elegant or pretty – the sort of young woman who would be a good choice for a wife. Whenever we were invited to a dinner, I brought a homemade dessert along for the table because I knew it'd be the sort of thing the aunties would remark upon in glowing terms and that his mother would hear. One Eid, I spent a weekend making plum jam from scratch to give to every aunty as a gift – an attempt to show how charming and thoughtful and domestic I was. (I know how desperate this sounds.)

Other families cottoned on, and my name and his were whispered as ones-to-watch. An old childhood friend I'd lost touch with texted me out of the blue, asking if what she'd heard about our potential pairing was true, and if so, she was praying hard for it because she'd always thought it would be the loveliest thing, for some of our childhood circle to be coupled off. For the longest time, I'd hankered after a love story and now maybe this was it. Maybe I'd be able to tell myself we'd known each other as children, even if the truth was I didn't really know anything about him at all.

Three or four months later, my mum phoned and said, matter-of-factly, 'It's okay, we'll look elsewhere.' His family had changed their mind; she didn't know why. Or if she did, she didn't tell me. And that, once again, was that. My disappointment unravelled into outrage as I shouted angrily down the phone, furious at the way all of this suitor stuff worked. I was angry at myself for playing along. I'd spent hours making plum jam, for God's sake. Later, off the phone and alone, my anger passed into something uglier. I wondered what it was that I had done, where it was exactly that I fell short this time. What was wrong with me? Look at you, I told myself. Pathetic, that's what you are.

In romantic comedies, this sort of thing was funny; always the bridesmaid, never the bride, etc. In real life, it was draining. It felt like everyone was so critical, pulling at me like a loose thread on a hem that was threatening to come undone. I was frequently told by well-meaning aunties (not known for their tact) that I was being too picky, that everyone has to compromise. In my family's circle, marriage was everything or at least it felt like it to me. It was all people talked about, all I heard, and I was nowhere close to it, and so of course it made me think that there must have been something wrong with me. That it was all my fault. Whenever I looked in the mirror, the first thought that came into my head was that I just wasn't good enough for anyone.

In Paris, all those years ago, I had been so hopeful about my life. I was on my way to discovering what it meant to be confident in myself, and I had found great satisfaction, a sort of happiness even, living on my own. I had plans, dreams, direction. But I didn't get to grasp any of it because then I came home and everything changed. Everything I thought I could be, I

116

couldn't be any longer. Meanwhile the lonely moments had started to accumulate, like lost change hiding in unexpected places, crumpled tissues left in coat pockets. I was so sick of it; the loneliness.

That was how, at the grand old age of twenty-seven, I found myself in a small windowless room in Clerkenwell, handing over £125 cash to join a South Asian matrimonial agency, filling in a questionnaire that quite specifically asked me how much I weighed.

LATE MARCH, 2011

Richard asks if we can talk, after the night of the super-moon. We arrange to meet for breakfast off Upper Street on a Sunday morning and somehow we end up wandering back into Tinderbox, where we began. It seems fitting to me that this is where it ends, too. I am convinced that this is what is going to happen. I am sure of it. KK says it might not be so bad. I say, 'Isn't that what "Can we talk?" means?' All morning, I steel myself for this moment.

'Are you okay?' He sits opposite me. He is frowning, concerned. He stretches his hands out towards me across the table, but my hands stay firmly in my lap.

'Yeah. It's just, I think I know what you're going to say and I get it, I do.'

'What am I going to say?'

'That I should have been more honest with you, and told you straight away about my family and the Muslim stuff.'

He stirs his coffee slowly and looks down and then looks straight back at me with a directness that is so steady, it is disarming.

'Well, it's not like I didn't know.'

'What do you mean?'

'It was right there on your profile. I already knew you were Muslim. It's not a secret, right? But it didn't put me off wanting to write to you. I mean, I might not know all the details but, yeah, I figured there might be something to . . . talk about.'

I am finding it hard to look at him, so I look down at the table instead. Everything is a little bit blurry.

'Look. All I know is that I don't want this to end without even trying, and I don't think you do either. So if there are things we need to talk about, things we need to work out, then let's do that and just see where we are, take it from there.'

I don't say anything for a while.

'Unless you don't want to?'

I shake my head. 'No, it's not that,' I say. I want to tell him I do want to, very much, but I have no idea where or how to begin. I want to tell him that I have never felt this before. It has never felt like this with anyone.

'See, what I'm trying to say is,' he stops and sighs. He shrugs a little bit. 'I like being with you. You make me happy. And I don't just go around telling girls that. I don't think it's worth giving up just because you think it might be too difficult. Like, you don't have to do it all on your own. We could figure it out.'

I nod. I feel as though I might cry if I look at him.

'So what are you saying?' I say in a small voice.

'Isn't it obvious?'

I shake my head.

'I really, really like you,' he says softly.

I allow myself to smile then, because I really, really like him too. But it is still only a small half-smile because I don't know if liking each other is enough to see us through.

We spend hours talking. I tell him everything, about the expectations and the rules of religion and propriety. I tell him about the arranged marriage suitors, the matrimonial agency. I wait for him to laugh, to back away with his hands in the air because I'm clearly a total nutcase. But instead when he walks me to the station, I tilt my head up towards him and he looks down at me and says: 'I want you to know, I won't hurt you.'

Still, I'm not entirely sure if he fully understands the seriousness of the situation.

'I think I have to spell it out to him,' I tell KK.

'What, more than you already have done?'

'Just to be sure.'

I send Richard a message:

Me: *TO BE CLEAR: If we want to be together, we will have to get married.*

Richard: *I know. I get it.*

Me: *And you don't think that's weird.*

Richard: *A little fast. But not weird.*

Me: *Huh. Okay.*

Richard: *Good talk, btw.*

Me: *I just wanted to make sure you get it.*

Richard: *TO BE CLEAR, I get it. I'm in.*

KK wants to know what he said once I spelled it out, again. I fill her in. She says, 'Does this mean you're kind of half betrothed?'

EARLY APRIL, 2011

Meanwhile, my mother has asked my eldest brother to help her find a match for me. It has been over a year since I've been introduced to anyone in this way. Up until this point, my brother hasn't been particularly bothered by any of what is going on with me, and it has actually been a huge relief for me to have someone in the family who couldn't care less about me being single (I mean this in a good way). But because my mother has asked him several times, he rustles up a dentist for me to meet. I think it's someone he knows from his weekly football team. I immediately recognise the name, the description: Ayisha has also been recently introduced to him. He was quite keen, apparently, but she turned him down.

I have the dentist's number in my phone but I don't want to contact him because now I've met Richard and I'm starting to feel happier than I've felt in a very long time. But my mother keeps asking if I've called him, the dentist, and she is becoming more and more persistent about it. I ignore her texts because I don't know what else to do; I don't know how to begin to tell her about Richard because we still have a lot to talk about.

One night she calls me and makes it clear that she thinks this dentist will probably be my last chance. Next month I will turn thirty, she reminds me, and it continues: I am being picky, I am running out of options, I am not a princess, look what happened last time. She is angry that I am wasting time, asking why I'm acting as though my mind is already made up. I am angry too, because actually I've been angry for years and I tell her I don't want to do this again and I'm tired of being told what to do. Everyone else listens to their parents, she says. Everyone else does as they're told.

'What is it you think you are waiting for?' she says, speaking fast in Urdu like she does when she gets mad at me. 'Who is it you think you deserve? You think you are someone so great?'

THESE DAYS

I still understand Urdu, but my spoken Urdu is broken and stilted. My clumsy tongue cannot wrap itself around anything beyond the basics of hello, how are you, I am fine. I can speak French fluently and yet I can't speak my mother tongue. When relatives call from Pakistan on Eid or funerals, my mother thrusts the phone into my hand and looks at me impatiently, urging me to speak in Urdu and not show myself up.

Thankfully this happens a lot less now. My incompetence only makes long-distance video calls even more unnecessarily embarrassing for everyone concerned. I am not proud of this and I understand it is a disappointment. When spoken softly, Urdu still sounds like poetry to me.

Sometimes I wonder if this duality of language is why my mother and I fall out occasionally, the way most (all) mothers and daughters invariably do. We don't intend for our words to be taken the wrong way but sometimes they are anyway. Most of the time, we talk in English (and don't assume she doesn't speak it well: she has a degree in it and once cited Hardy as her favourite author) but sometimes she says something in Urdu, I shoot back in English and so it goes on, our misinterpretation amplified. It is perhaps my misunderstanding of Urdu that results in the confusion, for when two languages crossfire, there is no room for the nuances lost in between just as there is no room in between right and wrong, good and bad, halal, haram.

When I eventually told my mother about Richard, I took her reaction to mean that she cared more about what other people would think than what I wanted, than any chance I had at being happy. But I was wrong to have given her such little credit. Her anger was only her fear, her worry of the unknown, in disguise.

I think about my mother's story. She had told me once that she had been engaged to another man before my father, bowing to pressure from her family to say yes. She had never liked this other man and found him cold and mean on the few occasions she met him as her fiancé. From somewhere, she found the courage to break it off even though her extended family told her not to. She didn't care what people thought, what they might have said.

When my mother first moved to England, a young bride herself, she had no way of knowing what it would be like to one day have a daughter who spoke so differently to her, whose ideas and dreams and education and expectations and points of cultural references would not be the same as the ones she grew up with. It can't have been easy for her, to navigate motherhood in a land so different from all that she had known, and so I understand why she tried to root me to something else, something that was hers: religion, culture, language, clothes, set ways to behave, guidelines on what I could and couldn't do. But where roots grow, wings fly; isn't that what they say? What I think my mother feared most when I told her about Richard was not what people would think, but that everything she had ever done for me, the act of raising me, stood for nothing. She didn't want me to uproot from the soil and fly some place unknown; that was all.

Telling my mother I wanted to marry a white English boy was a shock for her and maybe it even felt like a betrayal. Perhaps if I had been more trusting with her growing up, if she hadn't opened my post, if I had learned not to keep secrets, if I had had more privacy, if I had been more understanding, if we had both been less angry, if I was more like my cousins in Pakistan who were so well behaved and never spoke back, if the pressure to be perfect was not so intense, then perhaps the more difficult stages of life, the more difficult conversations we've had, might have been easier for us both to navigate. Perhaps it is the same for every daughter, every mother; for every woman in every family. I think of everything I could have done differently; I think of what we could have done better. I know now that all she wanted was to take care of me.

I think about my mother as a young woman, the same age as me when I went to Paris. I think of her putting her foot down and breaking off that first engagement because she knew in her heart that it was not right for her. I'd like to thank that young woman, whom I know from photographs was beautiful and graceful like a deer but must have also been brave, must also have had spirit, because she pushed back against one boundary so that I might in turn push back against a thousand more.

THOSE DAYS

The woman from the matrimonial agency sent me an email. *The headhunting has begun!* she wrote. She had found someone she wanted me to consider meeting. She sent me his details in an email, like this:

- *Twenty-nine years old*
- *Sunni Muslim*
- *Non-vegetarian (when there is no halal option, but does not eat pork)*
- *Non-smoker*
- *Non-drinker*
- *Educated with a master's degree in business management*
- *Occupation – business/financial services*
- *Lives independently (has his own place)*

In his photograph, he looked a little bit like a brown Mr Bean. The matchmaker asked me what I thought. I honestly didn't know what to say, so I said nothing. She emailed me again to say she had met him herself in person at one of her dating events. She told me that he was polite and open-minded and had a 'great personality'. She urged me to consider meeting him.

I mulled it over for a few days. I forwarded his profile to KK who just said sadly, 'I'm sorry.' I reminded myself that I'd paid for the service after all. I might as well see what would come of it, if anything. The matchmaker booked us a table at a 'fusion' place in Green Park and charged my credit card an extra £25 for making the reservation. I hated 'fusion' places.

I wasn't looking forward to it. I had made little effort; I looked a mess and I was overdue an eyebrow thread. He had come from work and wore a shiny black suit shirt and a thin gold chain. My lack of interest must have shown – and his did too. There was no spark between us, that much was clear. He flicked the tablecloth and kept checking his phone. We cut it short after mocktails, didn't even make it to dinner. When I left, I decided I would email the matchmaker and ask her to withdraw my profile. I didn't expect a refund.

It surprised me, then, to hear from him again, after weeks of silence on both our parts. He wanted to go for dinner. I declined and made up an excuse. But he persisted, texting in an annoying way: *So why did you join the agency then? Come on, it's just dinner!* I had run out of excuses and I guess I had nothing better to do, so I caved. We met at a restaurant in Borough Market. KK texted me.

KK: *Are you okay?*

Me: *Why do I say yes to these things?*

KK: *Can you leave?*

I should have left. I wish I'd left. I don't know why I didn't. On paper, he ticked the boxes of respectability and suitability. His family seemed so similar to mine in terms of our backgrounds: families in Lahore, our education, the way he talked about his parents' social circles, and I knew these things mattered. I told my mother about him and his credentials and she agreed that on paper there was nothing wrong with him. She trusted me to meet with him as long as it did not drag on too long, as long as he was clear that this was about marriage. I felt that with her trust in me, I could try and make it work. It felt like the best opportunity I had to get the whole marriage thing over and done with, once and for all.

'At least he doesn't live with his parents, right?' I said to KK.

'But do you even like him though?'

'I think I could . . . if I tried?'

Since we'd met in the context of a matrimonial agency I felt reassured we both knew what we were in it for. I felt better knowing that my mother knew about him, too. I thought it meant I was safe, somehow; that he wouldn't cross any lines, that he knew that we weren't dating but that we were getting to know each other respectfully, with marriage and an end in sight. (Or, at least, this is how I justified it to myself, even though it was totally obvious that it was *still* dating.)

There was something about him though, something off. I couldn't put my finger on it. He was flamboyant and popular, liked the attention he got from being loud, but he was also rude to waiters and didn't always look people in the eye when they were trying to talk to him. I began to notice these small things, such as how he hung up the phone at the end of a conversation without saying goodbye properly or always had an excuse as to why he could not meet my friends. We began to argue a lot. Then I realised what it was: he had a mean, spiteful streak. He pointed out all the things he didn't like about me and left me crying in the rain at Tower Bridge. He once cancelled dinner plans because he was going to an Asian speed-dating event instead; he told me it was sensible for him to keep his options open. I was so stupid I didn't even end it then. He went on holiday to Italy and happened to bump into his Italian ex from university there and they went for lunch. 'What a coincidence,' I said flatly as he showed me photos of her on his phone, though of course I knew it wasn't a coincidence at all. But I still didn't end it even then. Whenever we went for dinner, every time I considered the dessert menu, he'd ask me if I was sure, over and over, knowing he was making me feel self-conscious. Often he suggested I lose weight, said he'd prefer a taller, prettier girl, said that was what he knew his mother would like too. 'If there was one thing I could change about you,' he once said, as though he'd thought about it for an awfully long time, 'it'd be the way you look.'

But because now and again he promised me that he was serious about me and wanted to marry me and because he sometimes did things like look up wedding rings and wedding venues and because our back-grounds were so similar and because he had his own flat (which meant that if we did get married I wouldn't have to live with his parents, which at the very least was some small consolation, even if his mother had decorated his flat for him and chosen a hideous beige three-piece sofa suite with fringes and tassels on it), and because it wasn't as though he was horrible to me *all* the time and because there was no one else who was Pakistani and Muslim and ticked any boxes of suitability and because I felt as though I had literally no other options left, I let him say these things to me for months. I let him hang up the phone on me, let him check out other girls when I was by his side. At some point, I began to think that maybe this, maybe he, was all I deserved.

In the end, I had a lucky escape. I had been asking him for a while to meet my mum, and he eventually agreed. It wasn't exactly a traditional rishta scene. We met very quickly at Euston station before my mum caught her train home back to Walsall. He called her Aunty and talked platitudes in Urdu and that was that. To his credit, he was polite and well-mannered in those thirty minutes. But though we had both agreed to be honest with our parents, it turned out that he hadn't in fact told his mother about me at all. He had asked for photos of me to show his mum, promising me that he would talk to her. He thought photos of me would help; God only knows why, since he'd made it clear he didn't like my looks. Still, I picked out the nicer ones in which I thought I didn't look too bad – me at various family weddings in shalwar kameez. But his mum found the photos by accidentally-on-purpose going through his drawers and only then, when she confronted him, did he tell her about me as though I was a sordid little affair. He texted me and explained briefly what had happened. Then he said his mum wanted to talk to mine and so I sent him my mum's landline number and I took a deep breath and I thought, okay, even though his mum is a little angry perhaps now the mothers are involved, maybe we can just wrap this thing up. But it didn't exactly go that way. His mother called mine and exploded. She said she would never in a million years choose a girl like me for her son, a girl who was cheap and shameless enough to join this sort of agency and hand her photos out, as though I'd joined a brothel, as though those photos of me in shalwar kameez were pornography. She told my mother about her family's apparent social status in Ealing and how she would cherry-pick only the most beautiful of girls, from the best sort of wealthy families, and then she would choose one of those girls for him herself. She was already making a shortlist, she said. 'The girls who marry into our family,' she said, 'have something special about them that from what I see in your daughter's photo, she does not.'

I was stunned; I didn't know how everything had unravelled to this point, and he wouldn't pick up his phone. But I tried to make my mum feel better. I promised her I'd sort it all out, told her it must just be a misunderstanding, a big one admittedly, but one that perhaps could still be smoothed over if only our families or our mothers at least could meet. So I called him again, but he still didn't pick up his phone. I kept trying to call him. I tried for weeks. I guess I was hurt. I wanted to figure out what had happened and make sense of where it left me. I wanted him to tell his mother that I wasn't the sort of girl she said I was, that it hadn't been like that; I wanted him to tell her I *was* someone, that there *was* something about me. But he'd never expressed that much to me himself, never once suggested that I was more than enough for him, and so there was no reason for him to say as much to his mother on my behalf. Perhaps I wanted him to stand up for me. Perhaps I wanted to stand up to *him* myself. But he never called me back and eventually my mum put her hand on my arm and said softly, 'Just leave it. Just leave him.'

Once, not long after I had met Richard, I caught sight of the back of him in Liverpool Street station. I felt disorientated for a minute and then I watched him disappear and I thought, thank God he's out of my life. In a way, I'm grateful to his mother for that, because in the state of mind I was in back then, I might well have let him drag whatever it was between us on and on, because I felt I had no other options. Because I didn't realise I could take control. I don't know what happened to him but many years ago I had heard that a similar situation to mine had happened again – he'd promised a girl he'd marry her only he never did quite get around to telling his mum and once again, when the whole thing came to light, she put her foot down. I don't know if his mum ever found someone good enough for her standards.

Afterwards, my mother consoled me. She said his mother would have been an awful woman to have been lumbered with as a mother-in-law, and then she told me she had already known he wasn't of good stock. Not well brought up, she said. I asked her what gave it away. 'He didn't even offer to carry my suitcase,' she said.

~

Lovely Suzanne was getting married to lovely Mark and it was time for me to finally move out of my Sad Girl room in her house in East London and into my own place. I had taken a day off work to move, but the night before I couldn't sleep. I already had the keys so I snuck out of the house, loaded my two suitcases, which contained all the clothes and books I owned, into my car and drove to my empty flat just before dawn. I sat on the hardwood floor facing the balcony and I watched the layers of the morning sky, silver and pink and thin like watery icing dripping down the sides of a cake, and that was when I remember thinking: enough, now. Enough.

I had been so single-minded about pursuing marriage as though it were the only thing that mattered in the world that I could no longer see my own worth. In the process, I had forgotten who I really was, what I really wanted, who I could be when I was just being me; not a daughter, not somebody else's suitable or unsuitable match whittled down to a checklist of all the things I could or could not do. It wasn't just brown Mr Bean; it was all of them over the years: the doctor down the M1, the literary boy, the Saddam Hussein lookalike, the Fruit of the Loom guy, the family friends' son, everyone the aunties had ever suggested. The painful phone calls, the polite coffees, the profiles; all of them. All of it. The pointed remarks. The expectation from other people. The expectation I had put on myself. It was all too much and it had chipped away at me. 'Compromise,' I'd been told. 'You're being too picky,' I'd been told, by people who didn't even know me. It was always my fault, always something lacking in me. I was twenty-eight years old and this narrative had been going on for so many years that I had started to tell it to myself. I had started to believe it. There were times I called my mother after a Pakistani dinner party or a wedding and I asked her in desperation, 'Has anyone asked about me?' – meaning, does anybody at all have a son that might want to marry me? I wanted to be married so badly just so that this unsettling period of my life could end. I had spent most of my twenties feeling ashamed of being who I was, which is to say feeling ashamed of being single, that I had come to see myself as some sort of tragedy. I had begun to question all the choices I'd ever made, all the times I'd made sure I got my own way; the choice not to study something conventional and sensible like medicine or law, the choice to live alone in Paris, to take a job that paid a pittance and made me want to leave my dying father and move to London. And for what? To what end? By this point, back home in Walsall, every single girl I'd grown up with in our circle of family friends was married, settled, their parents smug and satisfied with knowing they had fulfilled their duty and their obedient, good, respectful children had fulfilled theirs too, while my poor mum was left with a reckless daughter like me. I was a leftover. The one nobody wanted. The one that wasn't good enough.

That morning, I sat on the floor of my empty new flat and I felt so drained, so empty. All I knew was that I didn't want to feel like that any more. I was so sick of it, of being judged by other people's mothers, of letting my own mother down. I was done with obsessing over trying to find someone to marry. It was time for that story to end, now. I was going to put myself first. I had to, because I couldn't keep on like this. I couldn't keep on hating myself.

My new flat was small, but it was mine. I had managed to buy it using the money my father had left me and through saving hard ever since I started work. It hit me that I hadn't lived on my own since Paris. A new-build flat in Colindale wasn't quite the same as living opposite the Seine, but it didn't matter. Because here it was again, a space of my own. The promise of something. An opportunity to begin again.

Slowly, I began to feel capable. One weekend, I woke up and decided to paint the entire flat. My brother offered to help but I said no – I wanted to do it on my own, and even though I couldn't quite reach the ceiling, and though in some lights the brush marks weren't quite as smooth as they could have been, I didn't care because I'd done it myself. I cut off all of my hair. I took up a weekly dance class where we learned routines to Beyoncé and I absolutely loved it. I went to Selfridges after work and got my belly-button pierced, something I'd always wanted to do when I was fifteen but had never dared to, would never have been allowed, but I did it thirteen years later just because I could, because I wanted to, and I didn't care that no one but me would ever see it or that it was perhaps, upon consideration, a little tacky. I bought myself a beautiful vintage writing desk and then, radically, I quit my job at the *Observer* and decided to go freelance. Though it was a big risk, it was one that excited rather than intimidated me. It took a while, and no small degree of therapy, but gradually I was able to look in the mirror and no longer see or hear what I thought other people saw or what

141

they had said: that I wasn't pretty enough, thin enough, tall enough, good enough, clever enough. Or if I heard those thoughts, I learned to try and ignore them, let them go. I felt as though finally, after all those false starts, after all that sadness, I was beginning to be on my way again.

After I moved into my new flat, after everything that had happened with brown Mr Bean, I asked my mother not to talk to me about the subject of marriage any more. I imagine she had had enough of it too. When I told her I needed a break from it all, I cried because I was just so tired, and she held me and she said softly, 'I don't know why you're in such a rush to get married. But there's no rush. You don't have to try so hard.' I remember feeling relief but also a great deal of confusion because I thought there *was* a rush. I thought I *had* to try. I thought that was precisely the whole point. But I was too exhausted to question it. So we both moved on, my mum and I. Instead of bemoaning my single status or lamenting my diminishing value as time ticked by, she drew a line for me and then stepped aside and gave me the space I needed. She took me shopping at TK Maxx for bright orange Le Creuset dishes and we spent weekends in John Lewis and IKEA buying bed linen and selecting fabric swatches for curtains. I fell in love with the idea of making my own home, somewhere just for me; shopping for soft furnishings with my mum was oddly soothing (and remains one of my favourite pastimes) and left me feeling surprisingly content. Sometimes I didn't want to leave my flat at all, but it was not out of sadness, it was not out of despair. It was because it was simply a place I loved to be. It became my home. I started inviting KK and Suzanne and our university friends over for regular Saturday night dinners, where we'd sit on the floor because I didn't have room for more than two tiny chairs; or else I'd call KK last-minute and we'd eat baked potatoes the size of our heads and watch *Glee* and dance to 'Don't Stop Believing', just because we could and we didn't care what anyone else who might have glimpsed us through my still-curtainless windows thought.

For most of my twenties there was a loneliness inside me. It stemmed from grief, but turned into something else. Whatever it was, it was ungentle and grasping, like fingers at a throat. It welled up inside me and rolled around in the empty expanse of my heart, rattling in the corners; it was there, always. I had thought that marrying someone in a way that was expected of me would fix it. Fix me. I had thought marrying someone, anyone, would untangle the knot that tugged away at my insides and sometimes made it hard to breathe. I had thought that if I had someone, anyone, I'd feel better; less sad, less lonely. Less unfinished. But that loneliness, that sadness, was all mine. I could have been at my own wedding, surrounded by my friends and my family's hundreds of wedding guests, and I'd still have been just as lonely, just as lost and raw and hurt on the inside. One night in my new bedroom, not long after I had moved in, I had the distinct feeling of the weight of a hand stroking my hair, but the moment I opened my eyes, the feeling had passed. Rather than being terrified, I felt a familiar sort of comfort and a strange sense of certainty. I don't know what it was, but I took it to mean that the loneliness was leaving and that somehow I would be okay.

In time, that tiny, sunny, pretty little flat and the balcony I filled with flowers gave me the warmth I needed. It became a place full of fun and friends, love and laughter, but also solitude when I needed it. I used to feel as though I needed an excuse to stay there on the weekends, at times I had to justify it even to myself, but I pushed myself to explain to my mother that sometimes I just wanted to be by myself and that this meant I might not always come home every other weekend. She understood. I listened to the voice that told me I was being selfish or inconsiderate – my mother was after all a widow, left unfairly alone through no choice or fault of her own, and as her only daughter I should have been there for her at every opportunity and I felt quite sure that this was what other people expected of me – but then I waited for that voice to finish saying what it had to say. I learned to be okay with it, not to let my guilt win.

Some nights, I unplugged the landline and turned off my mobile phone and it was a particularly delicious indulgence – uninterrupted swathes of evenings to do the simplest of things: read a book, cook, watch a movie, run a bath, write. It was in these quiet moments of solitude and those long weekends of pottering around in my own company without needing to justify it to anyone that I began to learn to be kinder to myself, to be less afraid of being on my own. I remembered the younger version of myself in Paris, how she was so very good at this; how exhilarating it was to feel untethered. I wanted a little bit of her self-belief, her sense of wonder. I learned to look around me and see how far I had come, how well I had done, and acknowledge that I had not failed, not at all. Perhaps I didn't need anyone else to fill the void; perhaps I never had. I made a promise to myself that if I did decide I was ever ready to meet anyone again, I'd do it better. I'd do it with the understanding that I was already complete. That it was up to me to make myself whole.

I had a full year off the arranged-marriage scene. I didn't plan for it; I didn't plan for anything at all actually; it's just that with time I stopped making marriage my sole reason for existing. When I accompanied my mother to weddings and dinner parties and other married women around my age, the girls I'd grown up with and shared a childhood with, sort of looked at me and my bare left hand with pity, I began to feel relieved that I had my own place in London to come back to. I had so much, even if I didn't have a wedding ring. I had articles to write and a desk to write at and I had friends who understood me. I had my own life. At some point, I realised I didn't have to organise my weekends around aunties and their dinner parties and all these weddings any more. So, I stopped going. Or at least got away with not going quite as much and my mum didn't press me on it.

It turned out that going freelance was the best thing that had happened to me, professionally. I had started to feel limited at the *Observer* and I was restless, bored of the consumer finance section I was writing for. I had no interest in writing about finance, and no background in it either. My plan had always been to get in, and then work my way across to where I wanted to be. I'd been pitching to other parts of the paper internally, and my determination started to pay off. Finally, I was writing for the sections I loved over at the *Guardian*, like g2 or life and style. The opinion desk occasionally asked me to write about being Muslim and being female, and about what it felt like to be put in a box, and even though those weren't necessarily things I'd have chosen to write about, I knew they'd help me get ahead. And they did. Through those pieces, people were starting to know my name. I had even collected my own faithful trolls below the line who referred to me indignantly as 'that Qureshi' – a sure sign of making it, or so I'd been told. But I could tell my desk editor wasn't thrilled about me writing for other sections; I would be reminded about something on base rates I was supposed to be doing instead. I felt frustrated at being pulled back when I wanted to run forward.

At the same time, I was overly self-conscious, caught between feeling invisible and not quite fitting in. I couldn't and still can't pinpoint why some mornings the idea of going into work unsettled me and left me with a certain dread in my stomach. Sometimes I felt painfully shy. Whatever it was, my insecurities multiplied around me. One of my superiors occasionally liked to drop into conversation how lucky I was to have got a job on the paper through the diversity scheme, though actually I'd applied to an advert, the same as everyone else. In fact, for the longest time I didn't know they'd had a diversity scheme because, in those days, you wouldn't have guessed it from a casual look around the newsroom. Once, an editor who sat two seats away from me and could never pronounce my name correctly despite my attempts to correct him made a remark about a new reporter and how well she fitted in, joining everyone for drinks, how she had exactly the sort of team spirit they were look-ing for. In my increasing state of self-doubt, I felt the implied comparison keenly: I didn't go out for drinks, always feeling awkward about being the only one not drinking. I wasn't sociable at work at all. I'd heard free-lancers describe working from home and it sounded like a dream because being in an office intimidated me; I felt more confident on my own.

A week or so before I left my job, the paper ran an event about diversity in the media and about four other people turned up. I thought, 'Enough, I'm sitting right here, I'm in the goddamn building', and in the heat of the moment, I sent an email to the big editors, the ones who called the shots, the ones who to me were well known and important and who I was therefore terrified of, and I said something like: *I'm here. Please take me off the consumer news desk and let me carry on writing the opinion pieces I've done so well at. PLEASE.* But the reply was simply, *Good luck! We're so lucky to have had you! xxx* I was fairly sure they must have thought I was a hot-desker or a temp fishing for a staff job.

When I went freelance, I realised that other people did know who I was. Those opinion pieces I beavered furiously away at in my spare time had set me up for something because other editors had heard of me. My confidence soared whenever I sent a pitch and briefly introduced myself and the reply came back as, *Yes, I'm familiar with your work, I loved your piece on xyz.* It was exhilarating, coming up with an idea on absolutely anything and researching it, realising I had a strong pitch, and then seeing the commissions come through. My bylines began to appear in the daily papers in all sorts of sections and it felt as though I was on a roll of good luck and – even better – the result of the hours I was putting in, sitting at my vintage writing desk in my sunny little flat, where I committed to wanting to be a better writer, a stronger journalist. Now I was no longer spending all my evenings either on halal dates or looking for them; I was staying up, reading and writing as much as I could, making notes, crafting pitches and waiting for commissions to land the next day. On a very basic level, not thinking about marriage all the time freed up so much mental space in my head, and this alone was revelatory. All of a sudden, I had nothing to distract me from throwing myself into my work. I had this need to prove to myself that I could do it, that I could be someone, and that I'd do it on my own because I was capable, because I was worthy. Because I deserved it. Because I wasn't who brown Mr Bean's mother said I was.

When my first piece made it into *The Times*, I burst into happy, smiling, sloppy tears because this was my dad's paper and I knew he'd have been so proud. The BBC called me up and asked if I'd like to audition for a weekly slot on the radio. It was only half an hour a week but I said, 'Yes. Yes, I'd like that very, very much.' Doors were opening and because I was no longer detoured by the stress and worry of finding someone suitable and getting married I ran through those doors as fast as I possibly could, back straight, head high.

It was around about this time that I met Remona, a brilliant Muslim freelance journalist whose work in the press I was familiar with. We were both invited to talk on a panel at the London School of Economics about being female Muslim journalists (a rare combination, much more so in those days). She slid into the seat next to me on the stage and whispered, 'Are there any hotties here?' with a wide, raucous smile and I warmed to her instantly. I hardly knew any other Muslim female journalists of my generation and it was a joy to find someone with whom I had so much in common, both work-related and otherwise. Remona was successful and intelligent, wildly rude and funny, and we hit it off instantly. She generously invited me into her tight fold of friends – mostly Muslim women in exciting jobs, who happened to be single – and I marvelled at them. I listened as they buoyed each other up and reminded each other of their successes, of their friendships, of the lives they made such a difference to just by being there. It's not that I didn't have this with my other friends – but I didn't have Muslim friends who could relate to the whole package of my life. It was different with my childhood friends because we had grown apart, or maybe it would be more accurate to say I'd never quite fitted in. I spent my childhood wanting to leave the little world our parents had created for us while it seemed they wanted to stay there forever. I'd never before met anyone who shared my background and yet didn't care about what other people might have thought about her choices or the way in which she moved through the world. I had always wanted to be that person but I'd been too scared. But the more time I spent with Remona, the more she showed me I could be free. It was as though I'd found a missing piece of myself.

I began to feel comfortable that this was who I was, this was who I wanted to be. I felt lighter, knowing that I didn't need to impress any potential husbands or potential mothers-in-law any more. It didn't happen overnight, but I began to carry myself differently, a tiny bit taller; I looked brighter, less worn down. At some point, in no small part thanks to Remona, KK and my mum, I realised that I was doing okay, some days I was doing great, and that whatever happened, whether I got married or not, I was going to be fine. Just fine. I had chased the loneliness, the unworthiness, away.

So you might wonder how it was, exactly, that I went from finally embracing being single and independent to finding myself alone in my flat a year later, signing up to Lovestruck, a new online dating site I'd seen an advert for on the Tube. Honestly, I don't remember what led me to that website that night. I don't remember writing my profile or paying my subscription. But I think that's the point. There was no crisis of loneliness then; there were no nights of despair or endless weeping over being single and unmarried. I saw the advert and I guess it reminded me that there were still possibilities out there if I wanted to find them. By now, I was in a good enough place emotionally to consider meeting someone to be an additional option in my life, not an absolute final end goal or a deadline I had to meet. When I signed

up, I didn't do it thinking that it was my last chance.
I didn't pin all my hopes on it because the more I was
on my own, the more I realised how much I loved
being on my own, actually. It was a relief – and I felt
incredibly lucky to be able to live on my own. So this
time around, I wasn't about to spend hours trying to
find someone who ticked all the boxes. It wasn't simply going to be about their identity. I wasn't going to
spend all my free evenings meeting every single guy
who just so happened to be brown-skinned, Muslim
and Pakistani. Away from journalism, I was taking
evening classes in creative writing. I started an inte-
riors blog after decorating my flat, despite knowing
nothing about blogging, and it grew into a sizeable
following of lovely readers who said the nicest things,
unlike my faithfully persistent trolls. I did yoga and
flamenco and I soaked up the richness and comfort
and company and love that my friends brought into
my life. I had a nephew by now and all of a sudden the
grief that had shadowed my family for so long lifted;
we had laughter and cuteness and cuddles. And most
of all I had, well, I had myself.

So when I signed up to Lovestruck, I did it thinking there was no harm; maybe it would lead to something, maybe it wouldn't. I was absolutely okay with that. I remember thinking there was nothing wrong with signing up to a dating website that wasn't specifically for Muslims because there were bound to be a few Muslims on it. I think I even thought it might just be fun. I didn't always reply if I got a message. Sometimes I forgot I'd even set my profile to 'live'. What I'm trying to say is that this time around, the idea of finding someone, making a suitable match, didn't occupy my every waking thought or haunt my sleep.

Until, that is, I got that first email from Richard and I thought, 'Oh. Well, isn't he just lovely.'

APRIL, 2011

Things are still tense with my mother after our falling-out on the phone. Now and again, I find myself remembering her words – that I'm not a princess, that I am being picky, that I'm running out of options – and when I think about what she said, I get a sinking feeling, a dread that sooner or later we're going to have to talk about marriage again and that we will probably have to keep on talking about it until somehow the subject resolves itself.

But on the other hand, in my other world, things with Richard feel good. It is such a relief to step into the world with him and I feel lighter for it. When I am with him, I forget everything else. Sometimes I meet him after work and we walk through central London and pick someplace to eat and we talk, and it feels right both on the surface and underneath, inside. One time, Richard says with great care, 'Would it be okay for you to come round to mine, for dinner? Would that be all right with you?' and I hesitate, not because I don't want to but because this is exactly the sort of thing I'm not supposed to do. But instead of feeling guilty, instead of worrying about it, I decide it is okay. I remind myself I am a grown-up and it's just dinner. He cooks for us. I help wash up. We fall into a routine. There is something about him that seems so familiar. I like the way that feels.

One Sunday when the weather is fine, we arrange to go up to Hampstead Heath for a walk. I am early so I wait for him on the pavement. It is a clear day, faint traces of clouds in the sky, and the sun is slanting. I am wearing a spring dress covered in tiny flowers and my arms are prickly with goosebumps so I move into the sun to warm up. When he approaches he has this strange, serious look on his face and I say, 'What?'

He says, 'Nothing, just . . .' But then he turns around and stops and stands in front of me, puts his hands lightly on my waist, and says in a very quiet voice with his brows furrowed, 'I think . . . I think it might feel like love', and all of a sudden I feel this surge, this force, rising inside me as though I might burst.

We meet each other's friends. He introduces me to his flatmate, his workmates, his two best friends. He meets KK; *He's lovely!* she texts. With KK, we take the train to visit Suzanne and Mark who have now moved out of London. KK takes a photo of us sitting on a bench at the train station, on a real camera, and it is the first picture of the two of us. Later she prints it out and gives it to me and she says, 'You both look so happy.'

158

Richard has told his parents and his brothers about me. 'They can't wait to meet you,' he says. And it is at this precise moment that I feel our bubble might burst because I can't say the same with any certainty. He feels familiar but he is also so different. He comes from a world where he can take girlfriends home for weekends, where he can show the world that he is in love with a big smile on his face, where he doesn't need to ask for permission. It is so easy for him.

It feels necessary to have some help. We meet up with a good friend of mine, Zara, and her husband Michael. Michael is also an English guy who converted to Islam and Zara says we can talk to them about anything, because she knows how hard it might be. I ask Zara how it was for her when she told her family about Michael. 'It was absolutely bloody awful,' she says, rolling her eyes at the memory. They broke it off, until eventually everyone came round. My heart sinks.

'But it's all right now!' she says, cheerily.

'Took a while though,' says Michael.

Richard asks Michael what the hardest part about becoming Muslim was. Michael leans in and says,

'Honestly? The washing after sex', and Zara wallops him around the head and tells him to shut up.

Richard has told his family everything about me. He has talked to them about Islam, explained to them the things he has been reading. His mother asked him if this was what he really wanted, and when he said yes, she said he had their full support, just like that. I wonder how I will ever be able to tell my family.

Ayisha already knows about him, because she's my closest friend from back home. We talk every Sunday on the phone, sometimes for hours; she confides in me about all the rishtas her parents are setting her up with, and so I couldn't not tell her about what's going on. She has some experience of this too: a female relative married a Welsh man and her very Indian family still aren't speaking to her. Ayisha has been trying to make the peace. She says, 'Whatever you do, don't tell your family about him until he's converted. Else he won't sound serious.'

I consider talking to Saba, my sister-in-law. I tell Richard about her. She is a lawyer from Pakistan and in true lawyerly fashion, she says what she wants and does what she wants. I am in awe of her. My brother and Saba met each other at a wedding. They danced together at a mehndi and it was blatantly obvious from that moment on that they were crazy about each other, orchestrating all sorts of ways to accidentally be in the same place at the same time. She got a job in England and they continued to see each other until their engagement was happily announced. They chose each other, so to speak, so their marriage was not technically traditionally arranged. But though it might have been what Bollywood films would refer to as a 'love marriage' it came with a big, fat stamp of parental approval on both sides. They married while my dad was still in hospital, and after his death, she brought us back to life. She fizzes like lemonade; her laugh is electric. Like Remona, she is clever and strong and opinionated and shatters other people's perceptions of what a woman born and raised in Pakistan might be like. She does things differently from everyone in Walsall which is why I know she won't judge me. One day, she rocked up to a family friend's lunch in

a short denim miniskirt with dark tights and she saw
the look on the aunties' faces and shrugged her shoulders and said, 'So what? I'm wearing tights! My legs
are covered!' and she was absolutely right and it was
a revelation. If anyone in my family will understand
about Richard, it will be her. I almost call, almost text
her to tell her about him. But then I hesitate. It feels too
big a step to bring her into this because she is family. I
don't want to implicate her or drag her into the middle
of things; it might make it even worse if the others find
out I told her before anyone else.

So I confide in Salma Baji, which is still a big step
for me because she is a family friend and close to my
mother too, but I trust her and she has perspective: her
sister married an English man whom she met at university decades ago. 'I'm here to help,' she says. 'Your
happiness matters to me, and I will do whatever I can
to make it easy. You're like my little sister.' On the day
of the royal wedding, while William and Kate kiss on
a balcony, Richard and I catch a train up north to meet
Salma Baji in a coffee shop in Leamington Spa, far
enough away from Walsall's prying eyes and anyone

accidentally seeing us. When Salma Baji sees us, she hugs Richard with tears in her eyes and says to us both, 'You look as though you belong together.'

Salma Baji buys us lunch and then tells us what happened with her sister. She says that though it was difficult, once he had won her parents over and proved to them that he was serious about converting and about marrying her sister, it turned out more than okay eventually. 'You just have to show you have the right intentions, both about converting and about marrying Huma,' she tells Richard. Salma Baji's sister and husband are happily married and the family fully accepted him. 'But what did she say exactly? How did she tell them?' I ask. But she can't remember; she wasn't in the room when it happened. It's this I struggle with and worry about. When the time comes, how will I find the words? And will they be enough?

⌒

One day, Richard calls me from Foyles in his lunch break. He is buying books on Islam.

'Don't do this for me,' I say.

'Of course not.'

Richard's grandparents are religious. They are Methodist and his father's upbringing was very strict. Though Richard's upbringing has not been especially religious, it doesn't mean he is irreligious. He buys several big, heavy textbooks (including *Islam for Dummies*) and later sends me a photo of them once he is home along with a caption: *Study time!*

I have not asked Richard to convert to Islam for me. In fact, I have repeatedly told him not to do it for me. If he does decide to convert, it has to come from him. I don't pray five times a day and I don't cover my hair but faith matters to me. It is in my heart. It matters to me that there's something bigger out there, that my father's soul didn't disappear into nothing. We talk about this. If Richard were to convert without conviction, it would feel empty, I think.

But since that evening in Hampstead, he has been looking things up. He finds a beginner's class on Islam at Regent's Park mosque. He asks me if I will come with him. I tell him I've never been. He can't believe this.

'Wait a minute, let me get this straight. So, it's really important that you marry a Muslim but you've never been to the mosque yourself?'

'Of course I've been to the mosque. I've just never been to *that* mosque.'

'How often do you go to this "other" mosque then?'

'Well . . . we go on Eid.'

'So you're saying you only go to the mosque, like, once a year?'

'TWICE! There are two Eids! Go back to your *Islam for Dummies*! Besides, I'm a woman. I don't even *have* to go to the mosque.'

I agree to go to the mosque class although I am sort of dreading it. My childhood experience of learning about religion was mostly dull; one of being told about all the things you couldn't do and that if you did do them, the angel on your left shoulder would write it all down and you would go to hell. I am not sure what someone from a liberal upbringing will make of it. But Richard has his books and has started making notes on his phone with questions. I dress carefully for our first class with a long top and a shawl to cover my hair.

I assume the class will be segregated and I tell Richard in a grave tone to expect this.

But when we arrive, I am surprised. The class is relaxed and lively; it is not segregated and though some women are covered, many are not. I look around. Everyone is young-looking, a similar age to us. Even the imam leading the class is. The imam is a short, stocky, friendly-looking man with a face as round as the moon and round glasses to match. He wears black robes and carries a Starbucks coffee cup. 'Rule number one!' he says. 'There's no compulsion in Islam!' This is a line I am familiar with but I have rarely seen anyone act this way. The way I have understood religion, you're supposed to be compelled. 'Too many people, they say you must do this, you must do that, you must never do this. But they judge!' He thumps the desk. 'Rule number two! Not up to anyone to judge!' He wags his finger. 'You can't make anyone do anything they don't want to do.' He leans back in his chair. 'Faith comes when you are ready.' He smiles. He puts his hands behind his head as if he's on that old Lilt advert. I half expect him to put his feet up on the desk. This is not at all what I thought it would be. I begin to relax. I begin to listen. I glance over at Richard and he is listening too, an amused look on his face.

Sometimes there are printouts and references to read. Mostly, it is the imam talking and lively discussion is encouraged. He likes to put things in the context of the everyday so that it all makes more sense. One time he says, 'If you're really hungry, and all you can find to eat is a non-halal turkey sandwich in M&S, then it's okay to say Bismillah and eat it.' A few of us laugh (I have never heard anyone admit to eating meat that is non-halal, something that is seriously frowned upon as far as I have been taught), but there are some concerned faces – they ask him if he's joking. The imam grows more serious. 'The point I am making,' he says, jabbing his finger again, 'is that people take Islam so literally they are forgetting that what is most important of all comes from the inside.' He jabs his finger at his own chest. 'So you eat a turkey sandwich from M&S, big deal. Allah forgives!' He shrugs. 'Islam is about being a good person. An honest, decent person. Islam is kindness, not guess who ate the turkey sandwich!'

Someone asks a question about interaction between non-Muslims and Muslims. 'Some people say you should not befriend non-Muslims. Should you shake hands with someone who is not Muslim?' The imam snorts.

'People, they say, "I can't say Merry Christmas, I'm Muslim." But I say, "Merry Christmas, everyone!" I say, "I'll be Santa!"' The imam chuckles to himself. Richard and I look at each other, bemused.

'So . . . what you're saying is . . . you *can* shake hands with someone who is not Muslim?'

The imam puts his head in his hands.

It is not all light-hearted. The imam talks passionately about the rights of women, the practice of prayer, the message of peace, the danger of some cultures taking Islam and twisting it into something else (he is especially critical of this), the rights of Muslim adults to choose whom they wish to marry. He puts an emphasis on intention; that if your intention is good, then that is all that matters, and this is something that I've never heard before. When I was growing up, I was not always sure if I was praying or fasting because I was being reminded to or because I wanted to; in these classes, I understand that faith can be private, personal and can't be measured in a performative way, which is how it has sometimes felt. His description of God is not terrifying or foreboding like the God of my childhood Islam lessons; his version of God is a kind, forgiving one who says it's no big deal if you mess up, who understands you're only human and that your best might not be perfect but it is still good enough. Richard too is surprised.

'You made out like . . . it would be awful.'

'Did I?'

'Yeah.'

'Oh. Sorry about that. I sort of thought it would be.'

'I get it though. It's values, I mean . . . at the end of the day it's just human values. The giving to charity – I get that, I really do. And the rest of it too. Being a good, honest, non-judgemental person. It's common sense, really.'

I say nothing.

'My grandparents might as well have been Muslim,' he adds.

'Imagine.'

On Good Friday, we have the day off work so I tentatively suggest we visit the mosque for Friday prayers. Richard doesn't know much about the Muslim way to pray and I figure this might be a good place to start, by watching. I haven't been to Friday prayers since I was a little girl, when occasionally I would accompany my brothers and my dad in school holidays because there was no one to look after me at home while my mum was at work. Richard says, 'Yeah, that'd be nice', as though I've suggested a picnic, and it occurs to me that with all of those suitable boys I had been introduced to, we never once talked about faith. As it is a bank holiday, the mosque is full and there are people everywhere, spilling into the gardens and into the courtyard under the brightness of the spring sun. We stand to the side and every single person says salaams to us and when Richard says it back for the first time I am a little bit overcome. The adhaan begins, and then I think, 'Crap! I'm in the wrong bit!' I gesture to Richard that I really should go to the women's side, but then I see that there are lots of men and women standing next to each other anyway. I am astonished when some of them start to pray side by side, rather than with the man standing two steps in front, the way I'd always been taught. A woman catches my confused expression and she smiles. 'If there is no room, it is fine. It is no matter,' and she shrugs as if to say, life is good. My shawl slips from my hair and no one yanks at it or tells me to put it back on in cross Urdu like they would at the mosque in Walsall. I am standing side by side with a white man who is not Muslim, who I am not married to and I am wearing jeans, not shalwar kameez, and nobody cares. All people do is smile at us.

After Sunday morning class, Richard and I walk through Regent's Park. Spring is warming up now. There are pink blossoms on the trees, the days are bright and pierced with sunlight. One day as we are walking around the boating lake, he says simply, 'Yeah, I think I'm ready.'

THESE DAYS

People who are not Muslim are always so interested, so surprised, that we are Muslim because he didn't change his name to an Islamic one (he didn't have to) and I don't cover my hair, and perhaps we seem a bit too relaxed about the whole thing, but honestly there is so much more to it than all of that. It is only because I was forced to relearn the basics of my faith with Richard that I have realised how it can be a private thing for us. We don't have to shout about it, is what I'm saying.

In recent years I have started to figure out what is important to me within the remit of faith and also what is less so, and I've come to realise that even if other people don't think this way, it's okay if I do. I have realised that I am drawn to an idea of faith that is more philosophical than the more literal interpretations of dos and don'ts that sometimes make my head spin. I'm not saying my approach is the right one; it is simply what makes more sense to me and though I'm clearly no scholar, I remind myself about intention and I try to do my best. What is in my heart is in my heart, and a top without sleeves or a summer dress doesn't detract from that any more, not for me at least. I have learned not to feel so guilty about what is on the outside because

I know it is what is inside that counts, and that's not necessarily for anyone else to see.

It astonishes me that some of the more outwardly strict Muslims are also the ones who, in my personal experience, are most likely to judge and point fingers. But then I check myself, because actually it's not that astonishing at all. These are the kind of people who disapprove of Muslims like me, the ones who look up my old *Guardian* articles on being female and Muslim from years ago and still, to this day, take the time to email or tweet me to wish me ill and tell me I'm not Muslim enough, that I can't just pick and choose the parts of Islam that please me and leave the rest; that it's typical that a woman like me should have married a white man because, they say, choosing a white man is a way for 'modern' Muslim women like me to distance ourselves from our own self-loathing. These are the kind of people (the men) who come to me and tap my shoulder when I'm at my father's grave and tell me I ought not to be there because women should not visit cemeteries (women are not, in fact, prohibited from this). In judging me and choosing to focus on the rituals

of religion alone, those who like to cast aspersions con-
veniently forget that it's not their place to judge.

After that Easter bank holiday weekend, when we
first went to Friday prayers, I began to teach Richard
how to pray. We stood next to each other and I recited
the Arabic prayers while he followed and it was in this
way that he learned what to do and how to do it. He
chose not to stand in front of me, as is normal practice,
and I know maybe that's not something every Muslim
will agree with, but it felt right to both of us. It was
the start of us figuring out how we'd navigate things
together. It was the first time I'd ever prayed in front of
someone who wasn't Muslim and all the while my heart
beat wildly, thinking – he's doing this, he's really doing
this. Though I still worried about the future, because
back then so much about our future was so unknown,
the more we did this, the more I felt this deep sense of
certainty that we were doing the right thing, in choosing to be together; that I was doing the right thing. We
don't pray five times a day but there are times when
Richard is putting the boys to bed and I'm tidying up
the mess the children have left in the bathroom and I

hear him saying Qul huwallahu ahad and something catches in my throat because I know that he doesn't have to do that, but he wants to.

There are still times when I panic, when I feel a certain pressure to make sure we raise our boys to know more about their religion than they do. It used to terrify me, that I'd get things wrong or that it wouldn't be enough in other people's eyes and then I realised that my motivation for teaching them about their religion was more to keep the naysayers at bay than anything else, which isn't the way it's supposed to be. So now, I'm learning to trust myself, and to trust Richard, and to know that we'll figure it out eventually even if Suffian looks at us shadily sometimes and asks us to prove where God is. I also know, in a way that I didn't before, that these are the sorts of questions that most children ask and that I'd rather he ask questions than not at all.

Still, sometimes it can feel as though people want to catch us out – does Richard really fast? Do I? Does he really know how to say his namaaz in Arabic? Like, all of it? Do we ever pray? I refer them back to our friendly imam's rule number two, and also rule number one while I'm at it. But I will say that if there is one thing that I can guarantee about Richard, it is that when he commits to something, he takes it to heart. He makes spreadsheets for finances and heart zone training and keto diets and, yes, even Ramadan.

MID-APRIL, 2011

My mother sends me an email about the dentist she wants me to meet. She writes:

> *Every time we talk, we end up fighting so I am picking up the courage to write to you instead. I get the impression you have rejected this suitor before any contact. Please look into it with an open mind. A lot of people know him and say he is good-mannered, intelligent, nice. He is well-established and there is financial security. I am always praying for your happiness. I love you more than life.*

My heart aches. I know she loves me, I know she doesn't mean the things she has said in anger because I haven't meant them either. I don't want to hurt her. But I know that by telling her about Richard, I will hurt her more. I just don't know what to say. I could keep stalling the dentist but I know it will only make things worse. Back in Walsall, so many of us growing up had learned to keep small secrets: boys climbing out of bedroom windows for nights out on the town, girls (not me) hiding miniskirts under their long school ones. Secret crushes, secret conversations, scraps of secret lives and tiny rebellions. All of us, even the best of us, had learned to tell little white lies. But I am so done with acting like I have something to hide. I wish I could be honest. I want to be honest with her.

Richard is up to speed on the dentist situation. I remember that I don't have to do this all on my own. I forward him my mum's email and ask him what he thinks.

He replies:

It's quite a beautiful email. If she's said all that, I can't imagine her ever being angry with you. She just wants to help in finding you happiness, particularly in view of what you went through last time. So I guess it's understandable that she'd feel a little hurt if she gets the impression that you're not willing to give her suggestions a try. Anyway though, I may be completely wrong as I obviously don't have much to go on, but I would think she'd be understanding if you tell her about us. If you're able to communicate to her how you feel about me as a person and how happy you are then surely she's likely to be ok with it? I'm sorry, I probably don't know enough to try to judge the situation so I hope you don't think I'm being too presumptuous.

I mull over his words. I consider that if everything happens for a reason, perhaps this is a door opening, an opportunity presenting itself for me to tell her about Richard and me. He is so hopeful that I allow myself to feel a little hopeful too. Perhaps he is right. Perhaps she really will be understanding. Perhaps it will be as easy as that.

I stand in front of the window and I look out at the clear sky. I ask myself if I am really going to do this. I realise that it's up to me, to write my story the way I want it to be. I sit down at my writing desk. I know that I won't ever find the words, unless I begin.

THOSE DAYS

When I was a little girl, there were a few daughters from Asian families my parents knew who were disowned because of the men they chose to marry. These were the daughters who had married against their parents' wishes, who moved away to other towns and cities, whose names were never spoken again. These were the daughters we were not supposed to become, not supposed to ask about. I don't recall the details now; I was so very young then. But I still remember snatches and scraps of their stories. I think one married a black man; that he was Muslim was of no consequence. Another, from an educated Pakistani family, married someone whose ancestry was from the more provincial parts and this, her parents thought, was beneath her, beneath them; a slur of sorts. Someone else married a man who had converted, but the fact that he was not born into Islam hurt her parents too much. She slipped away only to reappear sporadically and her family's hurt eventually healed with the birth of grand-children. From time to time, growing up, there were other whispered stories we'd catch while sitting on the stairs at some dinner party, snippets of other wayward daughters from other families in other towns who'd married for love. I don't know how their lives turned out but I hope they held on to the love they found. I realise now how brave they must have been, how hard it must have been to have lived with their love in the shadows, half in, half out.

When I was about fourteen, one of the older girls from our childhood circle became engaged to an English guy she'd met at university. He'd converted, this was made clear to everyone, and her parents announced the news with a great deal of joy and pride. It was the first time, I think, that a match like this was fully celebrated no differently from if he had been South Asian and born Muslim; I remember, because it felt so surreal. At the time, I had a major crush on a boy called James who lived across the road. He went to school with one of my brothers and came to our house sometimes to play cricket. I had braces and my eyebrows were the thickest they'd ever been and I remember staring wistfully at his bedroom window across the road after this wedding, the first of its kind that I'd ever been to, wondering forlornly how it was exactly that cute English boys became Muslim and therefore marriageable. I don't know how easy it was for this woman, who must have then been in her early twenties, to have told her parents about the man she wanted to marry, and I don't know how she made them agree or if she had to persuade them or if they were just okay with it from the outset. But because her new husband was so friendly and turned out to be quite religious and respectful to all the elders and went to dinner parties and celebrated Eid, their marriage helped set a precedent and a few more young women from our extended social circle went on to follow suit:

181

one married an Italian, another a redhead, another a blond.

But in spite of this, when it came to Richard and me, I didn't feel reassured. I still knew it wouldn't be easy and though I couldn't exactly articulate why, the foreboding followed me around. Maybe it was just my natural inclination to worry and panic and think the worst, or maybe it was because deep down I couldn't get my head around it; I could not, just could not, picture taking him home to meet my mum. In Paris, she'd almost had a heart attack when I bumped into a boy from my seminar who stepped forward to faire les bises with me as French people do (I stepped back to avoid him). Once, she'd come to London and a boy from work happened to be in the same Tube carriage and though I introduced her, she seemed uncomfortable, frosty even. She'd barely ever seen me talk to an English boy, so how could I tell her I wanted to marry one? In my head I played out the scene of me talking to her, but even in my imagination I couldn't find a way to start the conversation. Growing up we just didn't have the sort of conversations that might have facilitated this.

I hid letters; she opened them. I had learned to keep my doors closed.

I don't know how any of those other women (and it was almost always women) from our social circle navigated any of this because it wasn't something we ever talked about. On those rare occasions that a family announced that their daughter was engaged to someone who was not Asian, someone who had converted to Islam rather than coming from a Muslim family, the line was always that the couple had been 'introduced', using the same terminology as if it had been arranged even though everyone knew they hadn't, and the parents always made it very clear that the boy had been interested in Islam long before they'd met and didn't only convert for love.

When I was especially sad and lonely after my efforts with the Muslim internet, before I turned to the matrimonial agency, I remember once asking one of my old childhood friends, the one who'd married a blond, how she met her husband – but how they'd really met, not just the family-approved version, because I wanted to know what was possible. I wanted to know how someone might love you enough to change their life for you. But perhaps I crossed a line because she was far too coy and laughed me off, briskly. Even years later, we still weren't supposed to talk about these things – because good Muslim girls definitely don't date. Besides, once you're married, how you met doesn't matter. Nobody needs to know.

LATE APRIL, 2011

Dear Amee,

I know that things have been difficult between us lately. I know that we keep arguing over these rishtas and this dentist in particular that you have wanted me to meet. Sometimes I lose my temper and I am so sorry if I have upset you. He does sound respectable and I know that you only want what is best for me.

But there is something that I need to tell you. I have met someone and I would very much like you to meet him too. He is English and he has been learning about Islam through classes, and he is going to convert soon. He has already spoken to the imam at Regent's Park about it. His name is Richard. He has a good job and comes from a close-knit family. We've talked about the future quite seriously. Once he has converted, I hope that you might consider him, and approve of our match.

You might remember that a few years ago, I had tried meeting suitable rishtas online. Recently, I felt like it was time to try again. So that's how we met. I didn't deliberately look for someone who wasn't Muslim, it's just when we got talking we realised how much we have in common both in our values but also just as people. He has been very respectful.

I know that this may come as a big shock to you. I don't mean to upset you at all. Above all, I just want to be honest with you. I understand if you need some time to take this in. He has been open with his family about me, and it would mean a lot to me to be able to

185

be open with you too. I don't mean to hurt or disappoint you. I'm sorry if I have or if this does. I love you very much. I hope we can talk about this.

Huma

~

Richard comes over after work and I show him the draft of my email. It's important, I say, that he doesn't sound like he's just my secret white English boyfriend I've stashed in a cupboard. He reads it while I sort of stare at the glow of my laptop screen and then he says: 'I know I don't know her, but from what you've told me, I think she'll know that you've sent this with respect and love. I think she'll know that you care about her and you're not trying to make trouble.'

'I'm not sure she'll see it that way.'

'Whatever happens, I'll be here.'

At the very last minute, while Richard makes dinner, I decide to cc in my brothers and Saba, my sister-in-law. I figure everyone might as well know, now.

Before I press send, I find myself thinking of those women from my childhood and their different out-comes. The ones who got their happily ever after, the ones for whom life was not quite as easy. The ones who had to choose between the men they loved and their parents. I think about outcome A versus outcome B. I wonder which one I will be. A voice in my head keeps asking: 'And you, what will you do, if you have to choose?'

∼

As soon as I hit send, my insides tie themselves up into excruciatingly complicated knots. I find it hard to breathe. The next day, I can barely think. I keep refreshing my email. I don't hear from any of them. Richard tells me to stay calm, that there's no point thinking the worst when there's no way of knowing yet what's going on. 'She might need a few days to figure out what she wants to say,' he says.

I tell Ayisha. She sighs down the phone. 'Oh, Huma. What have you done?' She still thinks we ought to have waited until Richard had converted, but I tell her we didn't have time, we had to do it now because things were becoming so tense at home. Besides, I say, I think it would be worse if we waited. It would feel like even more of a secret, as though we'd been planning it all behind the scenes for months, when it hasn't been like that at all. I call Salma Baji in a panic, and tell her that it's done. She tells me to stay calm, to wait. But then a few more days pass and in these days I feel as though my throat is closing in; the air stands thick in my flat and I have this urge to get as far away from England as possible.

'Can't we just elope?' I say to Richard.

'Pretty sure that'll only make things worse,' he says.

I wonder what my mum is thinking. I try to guess and deduce only anger and hurt from her silence. I look at my phone again and again. Richard says it's impossible to know how she is feeling and pointless to try and guess. 'Call her,' he says.

But I'm too terrified, so Salma Baji calls her for me and then she calls me back and gently says, 'Look, she is a little upset. Just give her a few days and then give her a call. It'll make her feel better to talk to you. Besides, you will have to talk to her, sooner or later.'

Eventually I call her, my voice trembling. I don't remember what we said, but I remember blood pounding in my head, my heart cartwheeling in my chest. I don't know if either of us listened to the other.

My email has been read by the others too. The replies trickle through. They leave me shaking, stop me in my tracks as though I've been punched. Something cracks inside me and I say to Richard, 'What have we done?' But we've done it now, I've done it, I've said it and I can't take it back. I sob into him but I feel stranded on the shore. When the memory of my father is raised, the question of how I think he would feel, I feel as though I have tripped up and fallen hard on my face. Richard tries to be there, tries to help but he can't, because how can he? He keeps telling me we'll work it out, but he can't possibly know that we will and he can't possibly know what it feels like to carry this much, to feel this weight pulling on your heart. His family want to take me out for lunch at a nice countryside pub; mine can't even bring themselves to say his name. When I tell him how I feel, he holds me and says, 'I'm just so sorry I've caused all of this.' Meanwhile, I get a text asking me to come home this weekend. A family meeting is called.

I say, 'I'm not sure I can go through with this.' Richard's face turns even paler, his voice sounds strange. He looks at me, with urgency, and I know that what he's thinking is: 'Do you mean you can't go through with the family meeting, or you can't go through with us?' I know that's what he's thinking because I'm thinking the same thing. We only met eight weeks ago.

'Look,' he says, and he takes my hands in his. 'Even if it's not that simple, I know we can work through everything to make it all happen, make everything right in the end. I know we can.' I want to believe him but I don't know if I have the strength.

'How can you be so sure?' I ask.

'Because they're your family. They love you.'

But, inside, now I'm thinking, he doesn't even know them. I'm thinking, it's easy for you to say. I let him hold me and I want to stay there, in his arms, but he doesn't, can't, fully understand just how much trouble I've caused, just how huge this could be, even if he says he does. The thought of the family meeting makes my stomach turn. Why can't I just toe the line? Why is it always me, making trouble?

He pulls me to him, his hand passing gently over my hair, and I realise that this is the only place I want to be. My eyes fill with tears. One objection that has been raised is that I can't possibly be sure about him because we met only two months ago. On paper, in rational common-sense terms, perhaps that is true, although the argumentative teenager in me wants to point out that an arranged marriage would happen just as fast, if not faster. In every way, he makes absolute sense to me. I feel grounded when I am with him. He feels right in all the important ways, all the ways that matter, and in all the less important ways too. I know that we have a chance to make something really good together, even if I can't exactly explain how I know this, or why. As he holds me, I realise that toeing the line isn't the same as living in a way that is true to me. To give him up, and to give up the potential of a whole world we could have, the potential of who we could be together if we could be together freely, would break my heart and his, and for what, exactly, would this noble sacrifice be? For who? And that's when I know I have to do this. For Richard, yes; for us, yes; but also for me, so that I do not walk away from the chance I have to grab the life that is happening right in front of me, rather than letting it go again, giving it to someone else.

I receive a text. *Congratulations!!!! I'm so happy for you guys! I just knew that something great was going to happen for you. And it's brilliant that he's converting. Can I meet him soon? I'm so happy for you!* It's Saba, who has only just seen my email. Someone, at least, is happy for us and I'm so relieved I can't stop crying.

But I am still terrified by the prospect of this family meeting; I dread it all week. Richard takes the afternoon off work the day before, so that we can talk things through and spend some time together before I have to go. He keeps telling me it'll be okay, and he seems so calm about it. On the one hand, I still fear he's totally misjudged the seriousness of the situation, but on the other hand I know he knows what's at stake because he's seen what it's doing to me. I realise he's being strong, staying calm, for me because if I saw he was as worked up or as worried as me, I'd crumble entirely. I wonder – what if I could have a little bit of his conviction?

I leave for Walsall on Saturday morning. As I drive up the motorway my legs shake, jittery and skittish, and I can't seem to stop them, which makes for a mildly dangerous drive home. When I open the door, I feel nauseous. I mumble my salaams and then take my bag upstairs. 'I wish you were here,' I text Richard from my teenage bedroom forlornly, but the idea of him being here with me is of course a laughable impossibility.

At some point, my mother calls my brothers down into the lounge and we gather awkwardly. The television is still on, Sky Sports, and I take this as a small good sign – my future is not serious enough to turn off the football at least. I am fidgety, tense, and my stomach lurches as though I'm about to tip over. I sit on the sofa and make a silent vow that I will leave for London as fast as I can. 'It's time to talk,' my mother says. Apart from Saba, they all have questions but their questions

are so specific, they are impossible to answer. What
will I do when he wants a glass of wine? What will
I do when he wants bacon for breakfast? What will
I do when his parents bring out a bottle of wine with
dinner? What will I do when our half-English kids
see their English cousins drinking and want to do the
same? Have we even thought about how we will raise
our children? What will I do if he tells me to wear a
bikini on the beach? What will I do if he goes the other
way and becomes so religious, he tells me to wear a
burka? Why, when this boy I have met can do whatever
he wants and has grown up without any restrictions
from religion or culture, would he choose to willingly
submit to 'our' sort of life? How genuine is his interest
in Islam? Do I realise that if I were to marry him and
if we were to divorce, then that really would be it, my
chances of ever marrying again would be over? Have
I given any thought to what our family in Pakistan
will think? My father's family is deeply traditional; my
eldest uncle, my father's eldest brother, is like a grandfather to us, revered and respected by all the extended
family. His opinion matters. What will he say? I am

asked. Did I even think about that? This is not our culture, they say, on and on it goes.

I feel my energy drain away. Every time I go home, I am prone to falling back into my teenage self; I want to slam doors, I want to escape, I despair. But I can't let it show. I promised Richard I wouldn't. Richard is very different from me in that he is level-headed and calm and rational, all the things that make me feel assured and safe when I am with him. He thinks before he speaks, which is perhaps not something my family (myself included) are naturally inclined to do. When I leave for Walsall, he reminds me not to lose it, not to lose my temper, and to try to see things from their perspective. 'Reassure them,' he says. 'Show them,' he says. 'They love you.' So I try to focus on him and how our life, my life, could be. I bite my tongue, trying hard not to be sarcastic, trying not to argue indignantly that if anyone was going to choose whether to wear a bikini or a burka it would be me, certainly not them and certainly not my husband. I try not to tell them that I don't need anyone's permission to marry him because I'm an adult, because Islam grants adults the right to choose their own spouse, and I don't insist because I know this will only wind them up. It will only prove their point, which is that by pursuing this I am being utterly disrespectful.

But their questions continue and they whirl around my head and I'm thinking, this is too much, enough. Enough. My thoughts become louder than the questions outside me. I stand up. My legs feel leaden. I know it's too Bollywood to just say, 'But I love him', and besides they would laugh, so instead I say, 'Okay, look. You might not approve, but I trust him. This is my choice. All I'm asking is for you to meet him and to take this seriously because it *is* going to happen. I'm not going to keep justifying him to you.' Everyone goes quiet. I think they thought they'd knock some sense into me, get me to give him up and agree. I feel a flow of energy and I turn to my eldest brother and say, 'Remind me, did we have to have a family meeting before you guys got married?' Then I ask Saba, 'Did everyone get to have an opinion on whether you would wear a bikini or how you were going to raise your kids before you even had any? We didn't, right?' My voice is trembling, my heart racing, but I've kept it together. I haven't lost my temper. Saba looks at me with this expression of surprise that seems to say, finally! It is as though the lawyer in her has been waiting for me to stand up and fight my case, as though she's silently cheering me on, and she nods her head, and shrugs her shoulders and says, 'She's right, she's right.' Someone is about to start another argument and she says, 'Seriously, guys? Just leave her alone!' and I am so grateful to her. I walk away and I exhale.

MAY, 2011

It is far from over. Concerns continue to be raised. Messages continue to be sent, the sort of messages that make me feel so uneasy I delete them immediately, without even opening them, so that I don't have to see them sitting in my inbox. I restore them when I feel brave enough to read the words, holding my phone at a distance, squinting, as though that will somehow make it hurt less. Delete, restore, read; delete again.

One of Richard's best friends asks him, 'Dude, what were you thinking? Did you not know she had two big brothers?' and when he says yes, his friend says, 'Well then, did you not think what you might have been letting yourself in for? Do you not think this is, you know, all happening a bit too fast?'

It's too much. 'We have to do something,' I tell Richard, 'because otherwise this will just keep on happening.' From somewhere, I take control. I text my mother to ask if she will meet him, just the three of us, and somehow the prospect of this doesn't scare me quite as much as sending that very first email. She reluctantly agrees, on the condition that he comes to her. *Absolutely*, I text back. We are communicating only by text, sparsely, because she is still so upset. Though the circumstances aren't ideal, I'm relieved to have the breathing space. Perhaps it's still too soon for us to talk on the phone, still too risky that we might both say things we later regret. I don't know why but I have this feeling that, whatever we say, it has to be face to face.

Richard and I take a day off work and catch the train up to Walsall; KK sends us a message to say good luck and so does Richard's mum; Salma Baji calls me and runs through what we must remember to say. He has bought my mum an orchid and when she opens the door, he says, 'Assalam-o-alaikum' and holds it out in front of him. She takes it from him but her face is sombre. A dreadful feeling comes over me.

My mum gestures to us to sit down and I feel strange, like a guest in my childhood home. She is in the kitchen, clattering lids and plates and warming up dishes and Richard and I look at each other, sitting on the edge of the sofa in silence.

'Is she okay?' he mouths.

'I have no idea,' I say quietly.

Then she calls us into the dining room for lunch and I see the table is overflowing with piles of naans and platters of rice and at least four different rich, homemade curries swimming in bowls. It's only the three of us, but there's so much food and I'm about to ask her why on earth she's made so much but as I take it all in, it hits me that this is her, trying her best. She has done this all for me. She is doing this for me. She might not yet have the words to welcome him, it might still be too soon, too hard, but she has invited him into our home even if a little begrudgingly, filled our table with food she has spent endless hours preparing. She has done all of this to say, 'Please be patient with me. I am trying. This is just not something I was prepared for.'

At the dinner table my mother remains tense, her mouth firm and straight, and she avoids looking at me. We are all anxious. Richard nervously tries to make small talk and begins to ask her about a holiday I'd told him she'd recently been on (I prepped him with icebreakers), but she raises her hand and interrupts. 'No, that's not why you are here. I need to know what's been going on and what your intentions are.'

He clears his throat but once he begins to speak, his voice is steady and gentle. He tells my mum that he understands her concerns and he'd like to reassure her. He tells her he's been reading about Islam and has taken a few classes and it makes sense to him, the values, the similarities with other Abrahamic faiths that feel familiar to him. He clarifies that he doesn't drink, doesn't eat haram meat. He talks about the respect he has for people who fast, how he's looking forward to trying it himself when Ramadan starts. He tells her he is learning Arabic prayers and he's converting in the next few weeks and he says he'd like her to be there, if she wants, that is, if it's not too much trouble.

'I see,' she says. 'And then what?'

'And then I'd like to ask for permission to marry your daughter, if you'll let me.'

I burn up and my mother takes a sip of water and swallows. 'There's something I keep wondering about. Why did you contact her in the first place on this "website"? Why her?'

He clears his throat again and looks across at me. I look down at the table and I think: please don't say you just fancied me. But of course that's not what he says. 'Because I wanted to settle down with someone who shared my views on life, the world. There was just . . . something about Huma. It sounded like . . . we might have a lot in common, and then we started writing to each other, and then we met and, I don't know, it just felt right.'

I don't even realise I'm holding my breath.

My mum takes another sip of water, another swallow. She nods her head indiscernibly and says, 'Huma, pass him the pilau. Don't leave him with an empty plate.' Then she looks straight at Richard and says, 'Come now, you must try a bit of everything.'

THESE DAYS

Richard helps my mother with things like buying her insurance or choosing a new phone or getting a box down from the loft. He fixes her computer sometimes, though even he can never get the printer to work, and lays the dinner table for her on Eid. When he drops her off at the Tube station after she has come to stay, he always carries her suitcase.

I know what you're thinking. You're thinking: That's it? A few angry messages, a family meeting, lunch and then everything was fine?

Perhaps this isn't the ending you expected. Perhaps my story isn't quite as dramatic as you'd hoped it would be. Maybe you felt you already knew what was coming before you'd even begun to read it: brown girl meets white boy, white boy helps her escape her strict upbringing, and so on. If you're brown like me, I'm guessing maybe you rolled your eyes and thought: just what we need, another stereotype. Perhaps you assumed I must have had to run away to be with Richard or been cut off from my family or at the very least disowned temporarily, reuniting only once my children were born. Maybe you were expecting a story of oppression, repression, my personal trauma neatly spilled to fit a familiar-feeling narrative. 'God, these Pakistanis!' You might think. Or: 'Oh, man! Muslims!' I'm not sorry to disappoint you.

A week after that lunch in Walsall, when Richard and my mum met each other for the first time, he converted at the mosque by reciting the shahada. My mum and Saba came and afterwards the imam turned to my mum and said, 'I like him, I like him very much!' And then he said, 'Richard! My friend!' and gave him a fist bump. We were engaged two weeks after Richard converted, shortly after my thirtieth birthday, but not until my mum had called all my relatives to check which weekend in October they'd be free to fly to England for our wedding, as is the Pakistani way. It took my siblings a little longer than my mum to come around, and one of them took slightly more time than the other, but you wouldn't have known that by the time we were married five months later, let alone now. I think I understand why though. They were worried that in choosing Richard, I was closing a door on our upbringing, the choices our parents had made. Our culture, which our parents had tried so very hard to keep us connected to. These days, when I talk about our culture I do it without punctuation marks.

Sometimes I forget that Richard and I had only met in person approximately four times before that night under the supermoon in Hampstead when we first talked about religion, my family and marriage. I forget how fast it all happened, what a blur it all was. Honestly, I don't think either of us knew what we were doing but we jumped in anyway. So I guess you could say we met twice: once that day in Tinderbox and once again as newly-weds. Because that's when we got to start again, out in the open with nothing to hide. These days, in the evenings when the children are asleep and we collapse on the sofa and eat dinner and watch Netflix and I curl up next to him or he pulls me close, everything feels as though it's how it ought to be. As though I'm in the right place, because I am.

Maybe you're wondering why I wrote this, if our ending was so neatly resolved, if we got the 'happily ever after' that my friend Saima urged me to write about, whatever that's supposed to mean. I already told you my story isn't unique. I told you that, right at the beginning. But that doesn't mean that stories like mine, everyday stories of falling in love and growing up, arguing with your parents and then making up, sadness and joy and life in all its shades and nuances, the moments that give meaning to life, don't deserve to be told.

Here's what I would tell my younger self: know that yes, you can be with the person you love even if it's not someone your family would have picked for you, even if your backgrounds aren't identical or made to fit by a matchmaker or a well-meaning but thoroughly tactless aunty. Know that it can be done without having to choose either/or. Know that though it may feel dramatic at the time, and that there may be difficult conversations to be had, the sort of conversations you won't know how to handle because nobody has ever talked truthfully about the topics, things are easier because times are changing. Try to remember that things often have a funny way of working out.

But also know that there may be something important at stake, because there nearly always is. Sometimes it might feel huge and impossible, like navigating the discussion around circumcising your baby son when it's always been done without question, but your new, convert husband doesn't agree. Other times it will be smaller, almost insignificant things – moments that are lost in translation when your extended ebullient Pakistani family is gathered together and you're not sure if you quite fit in. Know that you do fit in, and he does too, because he's there with you in the first place. Know also that these moments are not insurmountable and that in time there will be fewer and fewer of them, as you make your way through the world, together. As you learn to say: We might do things the same, but also a little differently.

Know that whatever might be at stake, it is worth it.

～

For most of my twenties, I was unable to look at myself in the mirror without wondering what was wrong with me. It wasn't just about appearance; my confidence, inside and out, was a thin, papery wisp of a thing and it was easily torn. For the longest time, those years were shot through with an unsettling murkiness, mottled with grief and self-hatred and crippling self-doubt and such deep, wide loneliness despite the best efforts of my family, my friends. My reflection was a weird stranger on the Tube. I was too afraid to look into my own eyes and acknowledge what was bubbling away underneath.

At some point, after all those rejections and before I met Richard, there came a moment where I had to force myself to look. I had to learn to hold my own gaze steadily and ask myself what it was I wanted from life and what I was going to do about it. I had to learn to accept other people's rejections and criticisms and also to understand that their rejections didn't mean there was something wrong with me. I had to stop letting other people set my worth. I had to learn to not worry so much all the time, to be kinder to myself, to my mother. I had to find a way to make space yet keep my own boundaries. If I'm honest, I'm still learning. Eventually, somewhere along the line, I found myself face to face with all the versions of the girl I once was. I still think of her. I tried to do right by her. I think, I hope, I did. I guess you could say, I met myself first, before I met him.

~

It is lockdown, June 2020, and the world is not what it was.

We have created a schedule of sorts, to enable us both to work, and as part of this routine, Richard takes the boys to the park at the bottom of Alexandra Palace after their dinner to run around and play, while I stay home and write. Sometimes it works perfectly. Other days, less so. Today is one of those days.

I am restless and tired. My mind flits anxiously between the news and my to-do list and my work. The cursor blinks at me, sadly, from my computer screen. I slam my laptop shut, slip on a pair of worn shoes and grab my keys. I forget my phone or perhaps I leave it behind on purpose and I head to the park.

It is early evening and soft sunlight filters through the trees. Solitary dog walkers are out on their evening stroll, scattered friends and families stretching their legs. I scan the playing fields, but I can't see Richard or the boys. I pick my way through the path that leads beneath the trees, stopping in the dappled shade. I wonder why I didn't bring my phone, so I could just call him and find out where they are.

Then I see them, in the distance. They are already up the steep path that leads to the palace at the top of the hill. I wave and keep walking; Richard notices and points at me and the boys jump up and down madly, calling out as if they haven't seen me for months instead of an hour. 'Come! Come on! We're going all the way up!' they yell, or that's what I assume they are saying from their exaggerated gestures. They start running down but I am already walking up towards them. We meet in the middle. The boys bound around me, excited; they've invented some sort of game and they're in a rush to reach the top. I don't quite catch all of it; they have a habit of talking over each other. 'Okay, okay!' I say, and I smile because even though I guard my time alone, I am glad I came. 'You're here,' Richard says, quietly. I lean against him briefly and then together, lagging behind the boys, we walk up.

ACKNOWLEDGEMENTS

I would never have written *How We Met* were it not for the brilliance of Olivia Bays, my editor at Elliott & Thompson. Thank you, not just for being an excellent editor, but for also becoming a wonderful friend in the process. Thank you to all the other incredible women at Elliott & Thompson who have also worked on *How We Met*: Pippa Crane, Sarah Rigby, Marianne Thorndahl, Ella Chapman, Meg Humphries, Jill Burrows, Marie Doherty, Victoria Simon-Shore and Emma Finnigan. I am so proud of this book which I may have written, but which every one of you helped make what it now is. I have felt in such safe hands with you all. My great thanks also to Laurie Robertson and Caroline Michel at Peters Fraser + Dunlop literary agency, for being so encouraging and supportive of my writing, at every step.

Parul Arora, your illustrations have long enchanted me; thank you for making the cover of *How We Met* simply beautiful. I'm thrilled to be sharing this book's journey with you.

To my mother, my brothers, my sisters-in-law: I cannot thank you enough for trusting me to tell my story, some of which is also our whole family's story. Amee, thank you for standing by me always. This is for Daddy, too. To my Birch family, thank you for letting me tell a story that you too were a part of, and for always being so unfailingly loving and supportive.

There were many times I questioned myself in the writing of this book. To Saba Qureshi, Salma Jaffri and Saima Mir, thank you for continually reminding me I had to do it, and that I could do it. You urged me to keep going; that will always mean an awful lot to me.

In the writing of this book, I found myself remembering an awful lot about my time at Warwick. To KK, SK, SP and all my friends from back then, who find themselves within these pages and memories, know that I think of our time together with much joy.

When this book was still just an idea in my head, I found myself sitting in a cafe with a few friends who happen to be mums-from-school, discussing whether to write it. You all said that I should. Thank you, for spurring me on and for friendships that have brought us and our families together far beyond the boundary of the school gates. Thank you especially to Lindsay Booth, for planting the seed that led to this book's initial idea, and to the Piccadilly People, who of course are not really Piccadilly People at all, for letting me borrow the opening anecdote from your little boy.

Much of this book is about love. Boys, one day when you are older, I hope all of this might mean something to you. I wrote it for you, with all of my heart.

And finally, Richard. Without you, there'd be no story to tell. I'm so very happy that we met.